The Middle Eastern
Founders of Religions
Moses, Jesus, Muhammad,
Zoroaster, and Baha'u'llah

Also published by S. A. Nigosian

Magic and Divination in the Old Testament.
World Religions: A Historical Approach, 4th edition.
Islam: Its History, Teachings and Practices.
The Zoroastrian Faith: Tradition and Modern Research.
Judaism: The Way of Holiness.
Modes of Worship.
From Ancient Writings to Sacred Texts: The Old Testament and Apocrypha.

The Middle Eastern Founders of Religions

Moses, Jesus, Muhammad, Zoroaster, and Baha'u'llah

Solomon Nigosian

sussex
ACADEMIC
PRESS
Brighton • Chicago • Toronto

2 4 6 8 10 9 7 5 3 1

First published 2016 in Great Britain by
SUSSEX ACADEMIC PRESS
PO Box 139
Eastbourne BN24 9BP

and in the United States of America by
SUSSEX ACADEMIC PRESS
Independent Publishers Group
814 N. Franklin Street, Chicago, IL 60610

and in Canada by
SUSSEX ACADEMIC PRESS (CANADA)

British Library Cataloguing in Publication Data
A CIP catalogue record for this book is available from the British Library.

Library of Congress Cataloging-in-Publication Data
Applied for.

Paperback ISBN 978-1-84519-757-5

Typeset and designed by Sussex Academic Press, Brighton & Eastbourne.
Printed by Edwards Brothers Malloy, Ann Arbor, USA.
This book is printed on acid-free paper.

Contents

Preface

This book presents an academic introduction to the life and teachings of five Middle Eastern founders of religion – five individuals whose systems of faith, thought, and action have won the allegiance of millions. All believed to have experienced a personal encounter with the divine – a "voice" directly from the "beyond" – to proclaim God's message to the community or people to which they belonged. All attracted followers and opponents. Similarities in their religious outlook abound; but differences between the five pervade their approach toward society and culture, with issues of law, war, women, morality, ethics, the kingdom of God, life after death, and eternal judgment, distinguishing their respective beliefs.

An Introduction provides an overview of the political history of the Middle East based on four periods (Early, Persian, Hellenistic, and Roman) and a brief description of the surviving religious traditions of the Middle East (including a proposal regarding the nature of so-called "selected" individuals). Five chapter texts separately address each religious founder from the Judaic and Christian traditions in terms of the religious world into which each individual appeared; the traditional account as presented by available sources or evidences; the reliability of the available sources or evidences for reconstructing their biographies; and a critical assessment of both the sources or evidences and the traditional account. A concluding chapter compares the similarities and differences of the received divine messages.

I wish to take this opportunity to express my special thanks to numerous friends and colleagues, who not only stimulated my interest in this topic but also granted me the benefit of their discerning criticism. Next, I am deeply grateful to Deborah van Eeken, whose constant encouragement and invaluable advice was an inspiration to bring this book to fruition. I am also grateful to the dedicated staff at Sussex Academic Press in seeing this book into production. Last, but not least, to my extended family for their undying love, understanding, and support.

Acknowledgments

The author would like to thank the following organizations and individuals for permission to use the illustrations on the cover (the Passover seder table; traditional route to Calvary; The Kaʻba at Mecca in Saudi Arabia; Zoroastrian worshipers offering homage and prayers; Baha'i holding the sign of "Unity of Mankind" from their sources: Baha'i Community of Canada, BOAC (British Airways), Royal Embassy of Saudi Arabia, Richard Arthur Couche, and others.

Short extracts from various texts are acknowledged as follows:

Arberry, Arthus J. *The Koran Interpreted.* London/New York: Oxford University Press, 1964.

Holy Bible with Apocrypha. New Revised Standard Version (NRSV). Oxford/New York: Oxford University Press, 1995.

Nigosian, S.A. *World Religions: A Historical Approach*, 4th ed. Boston/New York: Bedford/St Martin's Press, 2008.

Nigosian, S.A. *From Ancient Writings to Sacred Texts: Old Testament and Apocrypha.* Baltimore, MD: The Johns Hopkins University Press, 2004.

Nigosian, S.A. *Islam: Its History, Teachings and Practices.* Bloomington, IN: Indiana University Press, 2004.

Nigosian, S. A. *The Zoroastrian Faith: Tradition and Modern Research.* Montreal, Canada: McGill–Queen's University Press, 1993.

Pritchard, James B., ed. *The Ancient Near East: An Anthology of Texts and Pictures*, 2 vols. Princeton, NJ: Princeton University Press, 1975.

Kitab-i-Aqdas: The Most Holy Book/Bahaullah. Haifa: Baha'i World Centre, 1992.

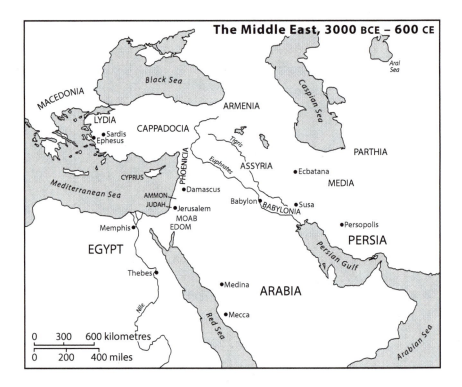

The Middle East, 3000 BCE – 600 CE

MACEDONIA

Black Sea

ARMENIA

Caspian Sea

Aral Sea

LYDIA

CAPPADOCIA

PARTHIA

●Sardis
Ephesus●

Tigris

●Ecbatana

MEDIA

PHOENICIA

Euphrates

ASSYRIA

Mediterranean Sea

CYPRUS

AMMON
JUDAH

●Damascus

Babylon●
BABYLONIA

●Susa

●Persopolis

●Jerusalem
MOAB
EDOM

Memphis●

PERSIA

EGYPT

Persian Gulf

Thebes●

●Medina

ARABIA

Nile

Red Sea

●Mecca

Arabian Sea

0   300   600 kilometres

0   200   400 miles

Excerpts from Sacred Texts

I (God) will raise up for them a prophet like you (Moses) from among their own people; I will put My words in the mouth of the prophet, who shall speak to them everything that I command.

(DEUTERONOMY 18:18)

Long ago God spoke to our ancestors in many and various ways by the prophets; but in these last days He has spoken to us by the son (Jesus), whom He appointed heir of all things, through whom He also created the worlds.

(HEBREWS 1:1–2)

Muhammad is not the father of anyone of your men, but the messenger of God, and the seal of the prophets, God has knowledge of everything.

(SURA 33: 40)

O Ahura Mazda . . . reveal unto me for my enlightenment that which Thou hast ordained as the better path for me (Zoroaster) to follow so that I may join myself unto it.

(YASNA 31.5)

Whoever claims to have a revelation from God before the expiration of a full thousand years, such a man is surely a lying imposter. We (Baha'u'llah) pray that God may graciously assist him to retract and repudiate such a claim. Should he repent, God will no doubt forgive him. If, however, he persists in his error, God will surely send down one who will deal mercilessly with him.

(BAHA'U'LLAH, KITAB-I-AQDAS, NO. 37)

This book is dedicated to
My extended family,
Especially to our latest additions
Dylan and Hayley

Introduction

The Middle East: An Overview

One of the most important areas for the study of human history is the Middle East the region popularly called "the cradle of ancient civilizations." Here, a number of ancient and modern peoples such as the Egyptians, Babylonians, Assyrians, Medes, Persians, Greeks, Romans, and Arabs, built great empires and imposed their will upon the territory's inhabitants. To be sure, there is hardly any racial, political, or linguistic homogeneity in the Middle East. And yet, modern Middle Easterners share a deep sense of pride in the history of their great past, particularly in their pioneering contributions of such fundamental innovations as agriculture; the domestication of animals for food, clothing and transportation; spinning and weaving; irrigation and drainage; standard tools and weapons; the wheel and metal-works; symbols of writing and keeping of records; astronomical observation and the calendar; mathematics; abstract thought; and many religious ideas and symbols.

Thus the entire region was, and still is, the scene of the most dramatic and decisive events in the history of humanity. From the existing archaeological discoveries and historical records, the political history of the region may be divided into four important periods.

1. Early Period (*ca.* 3000–559 BCE)
2. Persian Achaemenid Period (559–332 BCE)
3. Hellenistic Period (332–63 BCE)
4. Roman Period (63 BCE–CE 641)

Early Period (*ca.* 3000–559 BCE)

The earliest historical period of the Middle East is characterized by rivalries and struggles for supremacy and domination among the various groups of people occupying the area.[1] A number of city-states coalesced, either by force or by persuasion, to form a large political unit. Egypt was the first in Middle Eastern civilization to achieve such a political unification by about 3000 BCE under the rule of King Menes (or Narmer). Egypt's history from that point up to the Persian domination in the sixth century BCE changed very little, though internal disorders and external groups (like the Hyksos, Nubians, Ethiopians, and Assyrians) occasionally disrupted this unity. Native Egyptian dynasties continued to reassert themselves politically.

Moreover, by means of numerous campaigns or alliances, the Egyptians were capable of extending their power eastward to Mesopotamia (modern Iraq), northward to Asia Minor (modern Turkey–Syria), westward to present-day Libya, and southward to Nubia (modern Sudan). Egyptian trade and commerce with foreign ports were well developed. Similarly, Egyptian architecture, art, craftsmanship and metalwork were not only well advanced but among the best in the ancient world. Also, they introduced in the third millennium BCE, a calendar with a solar year of 365 days. Their most lasting and outstanding achievements, however, were the massive royal tombs (known as the Pyramids), the Sphinx (part of a massive mortuary temple connected with the Pyramid tomb), and the temples of Luxor and Karnak.

The history of Mesopotamia (modern Iraq) during this period is completely different from Egypt's. Here, the territory was exposed to continual invasions, and no significant unity was achieved (except for brief periods by neo-Assyrian and neo-Babylonian empires) until the Persian conquest in the sixth century BCE. During most of the twenty-four hundred years (from the thirtieth to the sixth century BCE) a succession of governments, differing politically and sometimes ethnically, developed what is called a "Mesopotamian" civilization.

The group of people living in southern Mesopotamia by 3000 BCE were the Sumerians. Their racial and linguistic origins are uncertain, but much of their culture, including their invention of writing, was absorbed by succeeding civilizations. About 2300 BCE, Sargon I, a Semitic ruler of a nearby city (Akkad or Agade), revolted against the Sumerians and conquered their territory. Sargon was one of the Semitic nomads who periodically migrated from the desert expanses of Arabia to the Tigris–Euphrates valley. He founded the dynasty of Akkad and established his capital in Babylon (modern Karbala). He and his Akkadian successors controlled and unified the region, including some adjacent territories. His political achievements must have been so great in his day that he was venerated as a hero for many centuries. During his dynastic rule, trading expeditions extended from Asia Minor to India.

Over a century later, the Gutians, a mountain people living in the region of Kurdistan, invaded southern Mesopotamia and disestablished the Akkadian dynasty. But Gutian control, too, came to an end after only a century when the Sumerians re-emerged under the new dynasty of the celebrated leader Ur-Nammu. Under his rule a highly organized empire and an extensive system of centralized control developed. The two most striking legacies of Ur-Nammu's reign were the *ziggurat*, a great, rectangular, stepped tower some 70 feet high erected in honour of Nanna, the moon-god, and a legal "code," the earliest collection of laws now known.

Several centuries later, the influx of another Semitic group known as the Amorites (or Amurru), the ever-recurring raids of the Elamites (perhaps of Alpine race), and internal racial rebellions finally crushed this neo-Sumerian empire. The result was the establishment of city-states governed by various Semitic tribes (mainly Elamite and Amorite) for nearly two centuries. Then around 1800 BCE Hammurabi came to power. A commanding leader and a capable administrator, he succeeded where others had failed. He welded the fragmented city-states of Mesopotamia into one kingdom known as the Babylonian dynasty. He gave the entire region one legal system, known as the "Code of Hammurabi," and one language, the Akkadian (old Babylonian) language.

Although this sociological pattern imposed by Hammurabi continued for several centuries, his military achievements did not long survive him. Once again, incursions of Indo-European tribes from beyond the Caucasus Mountains southward into Mesopotamia caused a great confusion.

The first group of invaders to strike Mesopotamia, shortly before 1600 BCE, were the Kassites, who eventually established a dynasty that ruled most of south and south-east Mesopotamia for several centuries. Other groups that conquered north-west Mesopotamia and were able to hold it in subjection for a few centuries were the Hittites and the Mitannis. The Hittites had invaded Asia Minor several centuries before; now during their expansion south-eastward, they sacked and looted the Babylonian capital. The Mitannis ruled a large, feudalistic area in Tell Halaf (the vicinity of modern

Syria–Armenia), where previously the Hurrians had been settled. And to add insult to injury, the Egyptians claimed south-western Mesopotamia and obtained tribute for a few centuries. Relations between these confederations were governed by elaborate treaties, which were constantly broken.

The ultimate beneficiary of all these confederations, or city-states, was destined to be the Assyrians, an insignificant Semitic tribe from Ashur (or Assur) in northern Mesopotamia. Meanwhile, the thirteenth century BCE saw the irruptive appearance of new peoples in the Middle East. The best known of the new settlers from the west were the Phrygians, the Lydians, and the Philistines.

For some time the Phrygians occupied most of the old Hittite area in Asia Minor, but later, in the seventh century BCE, they were defeated by the Lydians. The Philistines, who are considered to have come from the Aegean Islands (or, according to another account, from Crete), occupied the south coast of Canaan (Palestine, or modern Lebanon–Israel). They captured Canaanite cities and established a strong confederation of city-states. Nonetheless, they were constantly at war with surrounding tribes, especially the Israelites.

The Israelite invasion and settlement of Canaan around the thirteenth century BCE, inspired by their vision of the "Promised Land," coincided with the Philistine invasion and colonization of the same territory. Their timing could not have been much worse. It was little wonder, then, that their struggle to establish an independent Israelite kingdom was so hard fought.

The conquest of virtually all of Canaan by the Israelites did not become a reality until David's reign in the tenth century BCE. King David captured Jerusalem and expanded his territory to control everything from Syria to the Arabian desert, and from the Mediterranean Sea to the borders of Mesopotamia. However, this Israelite monarchy did not last very long. A little less than a century after its establishment it split into two. The northern part was destroyed by the Assyrians in the eighth century BCE. The southern part survived for a while, but eventually it too succumbed to the Chaldeans (also known as neo-Babylonians) in the sixth century BCE.

Assyrian militarism brought unity and even a degree of peace to the Middle East, but it was a peace based on terror. Once Assyrian leadership faltered, the empire collapsed. The coalition of Medes and Chaldeans destroyed the power of Assyria for all time to come.

Nineveh, the capital of Assyria, fell in 612 BCE and its site remains desolate to this day.

Persian Achaemenid Period (559–332 BCE)

Meanwhile, a new power was emerging in Persia. After defeating Media and uniting various tribes, a new Persian leader, Cyrus II (559–529 BCE), led his army victoriously into Asia Minor.[2] During the subsequent decade Cyrus conducted an astonishing series of military campaigns. His empire stretched from India through Mesopotamia to Syria-Canaan.

Questions concerning the historical roots and development of the Persians are still unresolved. All that can be said is that the Persians were a group of Indo-Aryans who ruled a vast territory in the Middle East for over a thousand years, from about 550 BCE to 651 CE. But the subject of the arrival and settlement of the Indo-Aryans in Iran is still a matter of dispute. It is generally held that the Medes and the Persians were the two groups of Aryans (from whom the term "Aryana" or "Iran" derives) who occupied and settled in the territory of Iran in the course of several centuries and in subsequent waves shortly after 1500 BCE.

The first Aryan people to make an impact in west Asia were the Medes. Sometime around the eighth century BCE they conquered the Urartu in the north, the Hittites in the west, and the Assyrians in the south and became the greatest power in west Asia. The formation of a Median confederation, or state, began when a certain chieftain called Daiukku (Greek, Deioces) devised a plan in 716 BCE for the union of certain tribal chiefs. But around this time the Cimmerians and the Scythians, warlike, nomadic peoples, appeared on the scene and caused serious disturbances. It was 673 BCE before Kashtaritu (Old Persian, Khshathrita) reformed a united Median state. Kashtaritu was soon defeated, but with the rise of Cyaxares, the united Median power grew greater than ever before, and the Persians, now in Persis, submitted to the Medes. A century later, however, the Medes lost their power and became subject to the Persians.

The Persians traced their history back to a certain eponymous ancestor called Achaemenes. But it was Cyrus II, a fifth-generation descendant of Achaemenes and a young prince of Fars (Greek, Persis, from which the term "Parsee" and "Persian" derive), who overthrew the Medes in 550 BCE and established the Achaemenid dynasty (550–330 BCE). In a short time he invaded the entire west Asian territory, from the borders of India to Greece.

The Persian takeover of power in the Middle East (starting with Cyrus) opened up new perspectives to conquered peoples. Cyrus and his successors not only respected the religious beliefs and practices of their subjects but also were prepared to support the local sanctuaries with funds from the royal treasury. The conquest of Babylon, Syria, and Palestine by the Persian King Cyrus II in 539 BCE opened up new perspectives for the people of Judah who had remained in Jerusalem as well as for those exiled to Babylon in 586 BCE. The policy of the Persian government toward conquered peoples in its vast realm was lenient, based more on self-interest than on kindness. Cyrus and his successors not only respected the religious beliefs and customs of their subjects but also were prepared to support the local cult, if necessary, with funds from the royal treasury. Instead of using the common practice of mass deportations, the Persian rulers allowed exiles to return to their homelands. The so-called Cyrus cylinder provides an impressive testimony to this policy, by which the Persian rulers tried to win the loyalty of their subjects. The inscription on the cylinder reads:

> I entered Babylon as a friend and I established the seat of government in the palace of the ruler under jubilation and rejoicing . . . All the kings of the entire world from the Upper to the Lower Sea, those who are seated in throne rooms, (those who) live in other [types of buildings as well as] all the kings of the West land living in tents, brought their heavy tributes and kissed my feet . . . From as far as Ashur and Susa, Agade, Eshununna, the towns Zamban . . . I returned to (these) sacred cities on the other side of the Tigris, the sanctuaries of which have been ruins for a long time, the images which (used) to live therein and established for them permanent sanctuaries. I (also) gathered all their (former) inhabitants and returned (to them) their habitations . . . All of them I settled in a peaceful place . . . ducks and doves . . . I endeavored to repair their dwelling places.[3]

Cyrus's extensive empire, consisting of widely differing peoples, cultures, and religious traditions, was held together by his innovative policy. He broke the tradition of victor as despoiler and avenger. Instead of invoking fire, the sword, the mass deportation of whole

populations, and the rigorous suppression of all nationalistic aspi-
rations among subjugated vassals, he conceded to the vanquished a
high degree of cultural and political autonomy, including religious
freedom. In other words, he accepted existing institutions almost
without modifications; he respected local traditions and adapted
himself to them, and he honored the gods of all the people within
his domain.

The biblical book of the prophet Isaiah (chapters 40–55) derives
from the period of the Neo-Babylonian captivity (586–538 BCE),
when many of the people of Judah were in exile in Babylon. The
prophet proclaims that YHWH is soon to free his people so that they
may return home to Jerusalem to begin a new life. This deliverance
is to be brought about by the fall of Babylon, the rise to power of
King Cyrus (Isa. 45:1), and the rebuilding of Solomon's temple in
Jerusalem (Isa. 44:28).

> Thus says YHWH to his anointed, to Cyrus, whose right hand I have
> grasped . . . I will go before you and level the heights, I will shatter
> the bronze gateways, smash the iron bars . . . For the sake of my
> servant Jacob and Israel my chosen. (Isa. 45:1–6)

Thus, Isaiah sees the Persian King Cyrus II as YHWH's agent
who would soon set the Israelite exiles free to return to Jerusalem
and rebuild their temple:

> Thus says YHWH, your redeemer . . . I am he who says of Cyrus,
> my shepherd: he will fulfill my whole purpose, saying of Jerusalem:
> Let her be rebuilt; and of the temple: Let your foundation be laid.
> (Isa. 44:24–28)

Did Isaiah have some knowledge of Cyrus's decree? We do not
know for sure, but he is the only prophet who gives Cyrus the title
of "messiah" (Hebrew *mashiah*, meaning anointed). In other words,
by proclaiming Cyrus a tool in the hands of YHWH, Isaiah
perceives the imminent fall of Babylon (Isa. 47), the return of his
people to Jerusalem and Judah (Isa. 51–52), and the restoration of
the temple (Isa. 44).

In keeping with his policy of conciliation, Cyrus II gave displaced
Jews the option, in 538 BCE, to return to their homeland. The book
of Ezra mentions Cyrus's policy.

In the first year of King Cyrus of Persia . . . YHWH stirred up the spirit of King Cyrus of Persia so that he sent a herald throughout all his kingdom, and also in a written edict declared: "Thus says King Cyrus of Persia: YHWH the god of heaven has given me all the kingdoms of the earth and has charged me to build him a house at Jerusalem in Judah. Any of those among you who are of his people are now permitted to go up to Jerusalem in Judah and rebuild the house of YHWH . . . and let all survivors in whatever place they reside be assisted by the people of their place with silver and gold, with goods and with animals." (Ezra 1:1–4; 6:3–5)

Many Jews made their way back to Jerusalem but were soon disillusioned and disheartened by the desolation they found. Their first attempt to rebuild the temple proved beyond their resources. It was not until much later that they resumed the task at the urging of two prophets, Haggai and Zechariah, completing it in 516 BCE.

Did the Persian King Cyrus II have any knowledge of the prophet Isaiah or of the religion of the exiled Israelites (ancestors of modern Jews) in Babylonia? We do not know.

Cyrus was succeeded by his son Cambyses II (529–522 BCE), who continued his father's work of conquest by adding Egypt and the Greek islands of Cyprus and Samos. Before his death the throne was taken by a usurper called Gaumata, who claimed to be Bardiya (Greek, Smerdis), the brother of Cambyses (cf. Herodotus 3.61–79). But his reign lasted only six months, at which time Darius I (522–486 BCE), son of Vishtaspa (Greek, Hystaspes) and a member of the Achaemenid dynasty, succeeded in securing the throne for himself after killing the Magians (cf. Herodotus 3.79). Next he put down a wave of rebellion throughout the empire. Then he crossed the Bosphorus in 512 BCE, subdued Thrace, and crossed the Danube river, but withdrew without consolidating these gains. Later, revolts in the Greek colonies of Asia Minor led him in 493 BCE and again in 491 BCE to fight against Greece, but in the end he was forced to withdraw to Asia Minor following the Battle of Marathon.

The political structure of the Persian Empire reached its fullest development under Darius the Great. It consisted of an absolute hereditary monarchy assisted by a central council of nobles and represented in the imperial provinces by local governors called satraps. In time, however, this political efficiency was overcome by corruption and civil strife, and the earlier policy of tolerance gave way to repression. The result was the gradual loss of confidence and alienation of subject peoples.

Xerxes I (486–465 BCE) succeeded his father Darius I and led another campaign against Greece. In 480 BCE he captured and burned Athens. But the defeat of his Persian fleet at the Battle of Salamis forced him to withdraw, and the loss of his cavalry at the Battle of Platea the next year consolidated the Greek victory.

Artaxerxes I (465–425 BCE) followed his father and reigned for forty years. During his reign, internal decay within the Persian Empire appeared in the form of revolts, first in Egypt and then in other satrapies. Also, intermittent warfare with the Greek states continued for a long time. Not until the accession of Artaxerxes III (359–338 BCE) were the earlier boundaries of the Persian Empire re-established for a brief period. The empire finally came to an end during the reign of Darius III (336–331 BCE), at the hands of Alexander the Great.

Hellenistic Period (332–63 BCE)

Alexander of Macedonia (356–323 BCE) first established control over the Greek mainland before setting out against Persia.[4] In the spring of 334 BCE, he stormed into Asia Minor with an army of 35,000 men, marched along the Mediterranean coast into Syria, then turned north and captured Darius' wife and mother. Next, he marched south into Phoenicia (modern Lebanon and Israel), captured Tyre and conquered Gaza. When he arrived in Egypt, the Egyptians hailed him as a deliverer, because they hated their harsh Persian rulers.

Then, Alexander turned once again to the Persian front. He met Darius III and his Persian army east of the Tigris River near the plain of Arbela (close to the city of Gaugamela) and in a decisive battle forced Darius III and his army to retire to the east. Darius III fled and was later killed by one of his generals, leaving Alexander king of Asia.

Babylon surrendered and Alexander entered the Persian heartland. He captured the city of Susa; burned the city of Persepolis in retaliation for the Persian burning of Athens; marched southwards occupying all the region ruled by local tribesmen; then turned northwards to Afghanistan, Bactria, Sogdiana, and the Hindu Kush mountains until he reached the rich plains of India in 326 BCE. The realm of Alexander now stretched from the Ionian Sea to the borders of north India. But in 323 BCE, on the eve of an expedition to conquer Arabia, he fell ill and died at the age of thirty-three.

Alexander's untimely death caused conflicts among his followers regarding the question of succession. Four of his generals staked their claim to govern a region of the empire. One ruled over the European territories; another controlled Asia Minor; a third held Egypt; and the fourth ruled Mesopotamia and Persia. The occupation of the Mediterranean seaboard became a matter of constant dispute between the Ptolemaic rulers of Egypt and the Seleucid rulers of Mesopotamia and Persia. Ultimately, the Persians regained their former strength. In 247 BCE Arshak (or Arsaces) revolted against Greek domination and gained the independence of the region of Parthia (modern north-east Iran).

The Parthians (247 BCE–226 CE) were a group of nomads who invaded and settled in Parthava (Parthia), in north-east Iran, sometime during the third century BCE. Soon they adopted the language, customs, and culture of their conquered people. In 247 BCE, Arshak (founder of the Arsacid dynasty) revolted against the Seleucids and gained the independence of Parthia. From then on, all the successors of Arshak, comprising in all some thirty-nine kings, used his name as a title. By the first century BCE the Arsacid dynasty (Parthian dynasty) had established their rule from the frontiers of India to the western borders of Mesopotamia (modern Iraq).

The Arsacid rulers set themselves up as heirs of the Achaemenids, adopted the old title "king of kings," transferred the seat of their rule to Ctesiphon and made the Parthian language (Persian written in Aramaic characters) the language of the imperial people.

A revolt which began in the city of Istakhr in the Persian province of Fars (Persis) at the beginning of the third century CE, put an end to the empire of the Parthians. A certain Papak (son of the priest Sasan, from whom the Sasanid dynasty derives its name) seized power from the local governor by a *coup d'état*. Soon after, Papak died and Ardashir (Old Persian: Artaxser, perhaps the younger son of Papak) succeeded to his position. Unfortunately our source of information on the lineage of Ardashir is scanty and conflicting. However, under Ardashir's leadership the rebellion against the long-established authority went swiftly. The fighting that inevitably broke out between Ardashir and the Parthian kings, Vologeses V (207–213 CE), Artabanus V (*ca.* 213–227 CE), and Artavasdes (*ca.*

227–229 CE), ended in victory for Ardashir, who now became master of the Persian Empire.

The Sasanid Empire (224–651 CE), which Ardashir founded, was engaged in constant conflict with the Romans. In particular, the hundred years of war between Rome and Persia, which began in 527, weakened both empires. Then, from the period of the death of Khosrow II in 628 to the end of the reign of the last Sasanid king, Yazdagird III, in 651, anarchy ensued, and various kings and pretenders followed one another. Yazdagird III was assassinated in 651 and the entire land of Iran fell to the Muslim Arab cohorts, who had penetrated into various parts of the Persian empire since 633. The victorious progress of the Arab conquerors was evidently swift and catastrophic. Indeed, the Muslim Arab invasion in the seventh century destroyed both the existing Persian and Roman political forces in the Middle East. Only a small territory in Turkey survived as the Byzantine Empire, until it too was ultimately conquered by the Turks in 1453.

Another group that resisted Hellenistic culture and civilization emerged from the Jewish people. In 165 BCE, Judas Maccabaeus, son of the priest Mattathias, led an open rebellion against the ruling sovereign, Antiochus IV, and recaptured most of Jerusalem. This period of Jewish (Maccabean) independence lasted till 63 BCE, when the Roman general Pompey, then stationed in Syria, occupied Jerusalem and declared the entire region to be a Roman province.

Roman Period (63 BCE–641 CE)

The rise and expansion of Roman domination from Italy throughout the Mediterranean world was a gradual process.[5] In 275 BCE Rome became the undisputed master of subjects and allies in central and southern Italy. In 148 BCE Macedon became a Roman province, and in 146 BCE Greece and part of north Africa were taken over. The growth of Roman interests in Egypt and the conflicts with the ruling powers in Asia Minor and other territories in the Middle East paved the way between 146 BCE and 50 BCE for a Roman penetration and extension over a large part of the Middle East. From time to time, Jewish discontentment against the Romans broke into open rebellion. Unfortunately, they were ruthlessly crushed. After a final unsuccessful struggle in 135 CE, the Jewish population of Palestine scattered throughout the Mediterranean basin.

The Romans had conquered Palestine in 63 BCE, and by the time of the birth of Jesus (*ca.* 4 BCE), their empire had imposed a political unity on the lands bordering the Mediterranean that greatly facilitated the spread of various religions. The first few centuries were critical times for Christianity. To begin with, a series of persecutions threatened its survival. Accused of holding secret orgies and charged with infanticide, incest, and cannibalism, Christians were tortured. Emperor Nero (57–68 CE) used Christian victims for the bloody Roman arenas. Other emperors, such as Decius (249–251) and Diocletian (284–305), employed ruthless measures in an attempt to stamp out Christianity. Christians not only survived those early trials but by the middle of the fifth century emerged as the sole state religion of Rome. The two emperors most instrumental in this development were Constantine (with his joint ruler Licinius) and Theodosius I. The so-called Edict of Milan, issued by the co-emperors Constantine and Licinius in 313, stated:

> We therefore announce that, notwithstanding any provisions concerning the Christians in our former instructions, all who choose that religion are to be permitted to continue therein, without any let or hindrance, and are not to be in any way troubled or molested. Note that at the same time all others are to be allowed the free and unrestricted practice of their religions.[6]

But the Edict of Emperor Theodosius (379–395), issued around 395, went further in prohibiting, on pain of death, the existence of any religion except Christianity:

> We interdict all persons of criminal pagan mind from the accursed immolation of victims, from damnable sacrifices, and from all other such practices that are prohibited by the authority of the more ancient sanctions. We command that all their fanes, temples, and shrines, if even now any remain entire, shall be destroyed by the command of the magistrates, and shall be purified by the erection of the sign of the venerable Christian religion. All men shall know that if it should appear, by suitable proof before a competent judge, that any person has mocked this law, he shall be punished with death.[7]

The early period of Christianity was characterized by the first signs of differentiation and schism within the Christian movement. Internal disputes began to threaten the survival of Christianity as the persecutions by the Roman emperors had never done. As the disputes gave rise to numerous heretical movements, the Christian church was compelled to formulate an official creed (statement of belief) and to canonize certain writings as sacred scriptures. Also, the political and linguistic division of the Roman Empire into eastern and western parts in the fourth century created a basic rivalry for the leadership of Christianity. Rome was the centre of the west, where Latin was the dominant language; Constantinople (modern Istanbul in Turkey) was the centre of the east, where Greek predominated. Inevitably, the Christian establishments in the two centres competed for leadership. The issue was temporarily resolved at an ecumenical council convened in Constantinople in 381 that established five important ecclesiastical provinces, better known as Patriarchates: Rome, Constantinople, Alexandria, Antioch, and Jerusalem.

Various decisions, formulated at subsequent councils, hastened the fragmentation of Christianity. The first major rift came in the fifth and sixth centuries, when, discontented with certain issues and unwilling to be dominated by Constantinople, the Christian groups of Persia (also known as the Nestorian Church), Armenia, Syria (the so-called Jacobite Church), Ethiopia, Egypt (the Coptic Church), and India broke away from the rest of Christendom. To date, all have maintained autonomous existences.

Another challenge that the Greco-Roman world had to face in the seventh century was Islam, the religion of the Arabs. Arabia was the scene of political instability and economic chaos. In addition, there were Jewish and Christian settlements in Arabia whose presence in the social and economic life of Arabia often threatened the trade and finance of the Arabs. Incessant warfare between the powerful neighbours, Romans and Persians, exhausted the military strength of even the most powerful Arab chieftains.

Although the influence of Judaism and Christianity extended throughout Arabia, the religion of the Arabs was by and large animistic and polytheistic. They worshipped whatever they found awesome and mystical. When the prophet Muhammad led an armed force against the Meccans, who carried images of two goddesses to war, he effectively put an end to all idol worship and its associated practices.

Serious differences arose within the Islamic community immediately after Muhammad's death in 632. The critical issue was the designation of a political successor only, since a religious successor to Muhammad, the "seal" of the prophets, was unthinkable. One faction insisted that the Prophet had designated no successor and that therefore they were free to elect a leader. Another faction insisted that the Prophet had designated 'Ali, his cousin and son-in-law, to succeed him. Eventually, several of his highly respected companions prevailed upon the Medinese to elect a single leader from among two of Muhammad's fathers-in-law. The choice fell upon the aging Abu Bakr.

Abu Bakr became the first caliph (Arabic for "successor") and survived for two years, 632–634. This leadership was maintained by three succeeding caliphs, 'Umar (634–644), 'Uthman (644–656), and 'Ali (656–661), after which the office of the caliphate devolved upon two powerful dynasties who claimed descent from Muhammad and the Quraysh tribe: the Umayyad dynasty (661–750), and the 'Abbasid dynasty (750–1517). The Ottoman Turks then assumed the office of the caliphate and retained it until its abolition in 1924.

Consolidating both the political hegemony and the religious heritage inherited from Muhammad proved difficult from the beginning. Abu Bakr's first task was to discipline rebel tribesmen who reasoned that their allegiance to Muhammad and their obligation to pay an alms tax ended with their leader's death. The success of his action against the rebels led Abu Bakr next to organize and direct several military campaigns against Roman Syria, all of which were also spectacularly successful. On his deathbed in 634 Abu Bakr nominated as his successor 'Umar, another father-in-law of Muhammad and also a member of the Quraysh clan.

'Umar improved on the precedents set by Abu Bakr, particularly in the areas of political administration and military organization. During his ten-year tenure, Islamic conquest and expansion outside Arabia spread into territories controlled by both the Persian Empire and the Roman Empire. His military expeditions into the Roman Byzantine Empire led to the conquest of Syria in 636, Jordan and Israel (Palestine) in 638, and Egypt in 642. At the same time his campaigns against the Persian Empire gave him control in 637 of the territory now known as Iraq and of the Iranian plateau in 642.

'Umar's plans for further conquest came to an abrupt end when he was stabbed to death in 644 by a Persian slave. But by then he had firmly established the foundation of an Islamic state – one which would express both Arab culture and Islamic characteristics. He had also devised two policies, one for the conquered non-Muslim people and the other for the victorious Muslim Arabs. The former were to pay taxes in return for protection and for the freedom to maintain their separate cultural and religious identity. The latter were to occupy newly constructed quarters supported by the taxes of the former.

Thus, a number of civilizations built great empires and imposed their will upon the inhabitants of the Middle East. On the whole, however, no permanently predominant people or group ruled the area. Rather, each organic group, differing in origin, in turn assumed a principal role, and left its mark upon its own phase of history. Indeed, the social, political, economic, religious, literary, and artistic contribution of each group continued long after it passed out of history. Most historians agree that modern Western civilization was heir to the social, political, cultural, intellectual, and literary legacy of the Middle East.

Religious Traditions

Over 350 million people live in the Middle East today. Of the various ancient civilizations that once dominated the arena of Middle Eastern history, only to succumb to internal and external forces, five religious traditions left records extensive enough to permit an understanding of the religious beliefs and practices. Those that survived to the present day are Judaism, Zoroastrianism, Christianity, Islam, and Baha'i.

Islam is the religion of the overwhelming majority of the population of the Middle East. It originated in Arabia when Muhammad (570–632) succeeded in converting the various Arab tribes of the Arabian Peninsula from polytheistic to monotheistic beliefs and practices.

Christianity is, relatively speaking, the religion of small communities scattered in most countries of the Middle East. It emerged in Palestine, then under the rule of the Roman Empire, when a Jew called Jesus (*ca.* 4 BCE–28 CE) was arrested and executed on the cross just like any other convicted rebel or criminal under the Roman administration. His followers then reported that three phenomenal incidents happened following the crucifixion: (1) Jesus resurrected after three days; (2) Jesus was lifted up to heaven forty days after his resurrection; and (3) ten days after the ascent of Jesus his followers were filled with the Holy Spirit and spoke in strange languages.

Judaism is the religion of a minority group of Jews presently concentrated in Israel, as well as in numerous very small communities throughout the Middle East (and in the world-wide diaspora). Its origin goes back to either the biblical Abraham (? 19th century BCE) or the biblical Moses (? 13th century BCE). As the people's liberator, leader, and lawgiver Moses developed the Covenant, previously established between God and Abraham, Isaac, and Jacob, into one with God and the Israelite nation (ancestors of Jews).

Zoroastrianism is presently the religion of a tiny ethno-religious community living in their ancient homeland in Persia (modern Iran). Its founder is the Persian priest Zarathustra (known as Zoroaster), whose ideas of one God, cosmic dualism, Satan, eternal judgement transformed the Persian polytheistic religion and also made an incalculable influence on other religions, especially Judaism, Christianity, and Islam.

Baha'i is a recent small movement that was organized by the Iranian Mirza Husayn 'Ali Nuri (1817–1892, popularly known as Baha'u'llah) at the end of the nineteenth century. Although it is a small group, its followers are attempting to establish a permanent basis throughout the world.

For the past two hundred years, historians of religion have been fascinated by the world's religious individuals who created the faiths that have endured for centuries. The study of the life and teachings of such individuals will give us at least the beginning of an understanding of the message they delivered, without the confusing complexity and diversity which appear in the later forms of the religion. Their place in the religious history of humanity is very special. And yet, no religion is wholly the creation of an individual. No new message has ever succeeded in shaking off entirely the influence of the faith from which it arose. Such individuals are dependent upon the past; but they are also at the mercy of the future.

Furthermore, the study of such individuals is not such a simple matter as we might suppose. Several basic difficulties must be recognized at the outset. First of all, it is not easy to free ourselves from prejudice when we consider "founders" of religion whose ideas and character are radically different from our own. We must avoid thinking of them as being strange, queer, odd, peculiar, or weird. Such words should not be part of our vocabulary. They are usually terms to describe someone else's beliefs, seldom our own.

Another important point is that we must be careful not to fall into an uncritical enthusiasm by making a hasty and superficial judgment regarding either our own or some other special messenger. An objective study demands a combination in due proportion of a critical and sympathetic understanding.

Achieving the right attitude to study the life and teaching of "founders" is not the only difficulty; we must also secure reliable information. This too is by no means easy because complete and trustworthy biographies of such individuals are extremely scarce. Most of the information comes from writings that are very old and have passed through a long process of oral transmission, often involving considerable alteration from time to time. Even so, in most cases, they do not go back to the times of which they tell. The stories they contain are often handed down by word of mouth for centuries before they are put into writing. Consequently history and legend are inextricably tangled together. To know how much the stories contain historical facts and how much they are the result of pious imagination is extremely difficult. Still, we must realize that in every unhistorical element in the traditions there may be some real value – both religious and historical. A legend often reflects faithfully the real character of its hero. Even if the biography represented by tradition is unhistorical, it is the personality actually recognized by the adherents of the religion. As a matter of fact, the individual in whom the adherents of a religion believe is the individual presented by the legends. To understand the religion one must know the picture of the individual given by the accepted traditions.

The following chapters will present five Middle Eastern individuals namely, Moses, Jesus, Muhammad, Zoroaster, and Baha'u'llah, all of whom experienced several "divine encounters."

Mani (216–276 CE), another individual who lived in the Middle East and showed a genius for organization and created his own religious movement, will not be included in our list.[8] The scanty evidence we posses about Mani indicates that although he spent most of his time teaching his ideas, his privileged position was threatened by the Zoroastrian chief priest who finally instigated his torture and execution at the age of 60.

At the time of Mani's death, his religion had evolved into a highly organized system that had spread beyond the borders of the Roman Empire into Arabia, Iran, India, and China. Nothing is known for certain about the introduction and spread of Manichaeism in the Roman Empire except for the evidence that it reached beyond Iran to Egypt, northern Africa, and Spain and from Syria to Turkey, Greece, Italy, and France. Its prevalence is attested to by the determined opposition of the Christian emperors who showed as much intolerance toward Manichaeism as did Iranian rulers. Emperor Diocletian, for instance, drew up an edict against the Manicheans in 297. His prescriptions were draconian: all Manichean written materials and their authors, along with all ringleaders, were to be burned; all adherents were to be put to death and their properties confiscated; and anyone who held a position of high rank or status in society and was found to follow the Manichean religion was to be condemned to a fate far worse than death – compulsory labour in the mines. Opposition to Manicheans was no less vigorous from Christian leaders. Christian writers from Syria, Iraq, and Armenia allude to the Manichean religion as a "dangerous, wicked" faith. Greek and Latin authors considered the Manichean religion an "insane heresy," that is, opposed to established dogma.

By far the most celebrated of Western authorities on Manichaeism was Augustine of Hippo (354–430), who for nine years (373–382) before his conversion to Christianity had been a professed Manichean. After his conversion, Augustine wrote several works arguing against Manicheans. Pope Leo I (440–461) played an especially prominent part in the persecution of the Manicheans. Little is known about the history of Manichaeism in Europe after the sixth century, because by that time the term "Manichean" had come to be used loosely to designate any heretical group. Unfortunately the ruthless measures adopted against Manicheans put an end to all future developments. Their recovery or survival seems very unlikely.

So, in the following pages we shall concentrate on the five individuals mentioned above, who actively proclaimed their religious perceptions and experiences as eternal truths. They will be divided into two groups: Moses, Jesus, and Muhammad, who are considered by some (but not all) to have in common "Abraham" as their ancestor; and Zoroaster, and Baha'u'llah, who lived in a common territory called Persia/Iran.

CHOSEN INDIVIDUALS: A CHRONOLOGY
(All Dates are Approximate)

Name and Date of Individual	Country of Birth	Name of Scripture(s) Date Compiled	Name of Religion Distribution
Moses (? 15th–13th cent. BCE)	Egypt	Torah (c.400 BCE)	Judaism Israel, Diaspora
Zoroaster (? 13th–6th cent. BCE)	Persia	Avesta (c.370 CE)	Zoroastrianism Iran, India, Diaspora
Jesus (c. 4 BCE–29 CE)	Palestine	New Testament (c. 397 CE)	Christianity Universal
Mani (216–277 CE)	Iraq	Seven Texts	Manichaeism Extinct
Muhammad (c. 571–632 CE)	Arabia	Qur'an (c. 650 CE)	Islam Universal
Baha'u'llah (1817–1892 CE)	Iran	Kitab-i-Aqdas (1873 CE)	Baha'i Widespread

BCE = Before the Common Era.; CE = Common Era.; c.= *circa* (about);
cent. = century

1
Moses

And the angel of the Lord appeared to him in a flame of fire out of the midst of a bush; and he looked, and lo, the bush was burning, yet it was not consumed. And Moses said, "I will turn aside and see this great sight, why the bush is not burnt." When the Lord (YHWH) saw that he turned aside to see, God (Elohim) called to him out of the bush, "Moses, Moses!" And he said, "Here am I." Then he [God] said, "Do not come closer; put off your shoes from your feet, for the place on which you are standing is holy ground."

(EXODUS 3:2–5)

Judaism is one of the oldest surviving religions that originated in the Middle East sometime during the middle of the second millennium BCE. It is practiced today by millions of Jews living in Israel and all over the world. To understand the religion of Judaism, we need to keep in mind the following important points.

First, Jews consider themselves direct descendants of Abraham, with whom God established a "Covenant." The significance of that concept is clear: Jews consider Judaism an extension of biblical religion and think of themselves as successors or inheritors of the "Chosen People" recorded in the Jewish scriptures (known as the Old Testament by Christians). From biblical days to the modern period, historical events have always been understood in terms of that unique Covenant between God and the Jewish people.

Second, Judaism has no identifiable founder analogous to most other religions (e.g., Buddhism, Christianity, Islam). The Jewish people consider Abraham their ancestral "father" who obeyed the divine command and Moses the one who received and transmitted the "divine Law" ("Instruction" or "Guidance").

Thus, the story of Moses has played a major role in the formation of Judaism and the Israelite nation (ancestors of Jews). As the people's liberator, leader, and lawgiver, he delivered the divine laws which formed the basis of Judaism. As lawgiver and founder of the Israelite nation, he developed the covenant, previously established between God and the patriarchs (Abraham Isaac, and Jacob), into one between God and the nation. More about that later; but first it is necessary to present the world into which Moses appeared.

Egypt: The Religious World of Moses

Long before the advent of the pharaohs, the Egyptians were already an ancient people with roots in the Old Stone Age, when scattered groups of hunters wandered along the mud strip of the Nile River. Some time between 10,000 and 7000 BCE, a pastoral group settled along the fertile Nile valley. Between 7000 and 3000 BCE, those settlers organized themselves into independent villages with buildings constructed of wood, brick, and stone. By about 3000 BCE they had developed the art of hieroglyphic writing (picture script), an advance followed shortly afterward by the unification of many village communities into a single kingdom under one imperial ruler, called the "pharaoh."[1]

From about 3000 BCE, the official religion recognized every pharaoh as the incarnate son of the sun god and a god himself. It was unnecessary, then, to seek the will or the mandate of the sun god, because that mandate was expressed through the pharaoh-god. Justice was based not on a code of laws but on the pharaoh's own decisions made in accordance with custom. Those who resisted the pharaoh's supreme authority were punished as rebels.

The cult of the pharaoh was perhaps best expressed by the immense structure of the pyramids.[2] Each pharaoh built a pyramid complex, which was both a symbol of his power and his final resting place. The divine tombs were central to the cult of the pharaoh-god, who in death was assumed to have returned to the company of all pharaoh-gods as the next pharaoh-god succeeded to his earthly mandate. The sight of those monuments suggested to the Greek invaders, centuries later, harsh, forced labour imposed by a hateful tyrant. Such a view was a misunderstanding of the religious conviction and mentality of the Egyptians, who willingly accepted the obligation to work on monumental projects as service befitting the incarnate pharaoh-god.

Along with the pharaoh cult, Egyptian religion embraced a remarkable variety of gods and goddesses.[3] Each region in Egypt had its own deity, and cities and villages in each region recognized local extensions to regional pantheons. The most striking feature of Egyptian religious tradition, however, was not its polytheistic nature or sheer quantity of gods; rather, Egyptian religion was distinguished by the remarkable qualities of its deities. Egyptian gods and goddesses were thought of either as complete animals or as semi-human and semi-animal forms.[4] Whatever the underlying concept, the Egyptians saw no difficulty in the worship of powers with human or animal characteristics.

Besides the deities endowed with animal forms, Egyptian religion recognized a host of other divinities. Among them were various cosmic deities, such as the earth god Geb, the heaven goddess Nut, and the air god Shu (note the reversal of the usual assignment of the sexes in ancient religions – a male earth god and a female god of heaven). Among the astral deities, the sun god Horus initially was the most prominent. He was not the only sun god, however; others were Kheprer, Atum, and Re (or Ra), who in time eclipsed Horus.

Attempts by the priests to organize this amorphous collection of deities and beliefs into some sort of system resulted in a variety of family groupings.[5] Some deities, such as the creator god Ptah, the war goddess Sekhmet, and the medicine god Imhotep, were identified in a triad as father, mother, and son, as were the sun god Amon-Re, the Nile goddess Mut, and their son, the moon god Khonsu.

No grouping of deities stirred popular interest more than the family that included the Isis–Osiris–Horus group.[6] According to the earliest Egyptian version of the story (the Pyramid Texts, assembled from fragments of funerary hymns and rituals), Osiris was a good and beneficent god-king who was killed by his evil brother, Seth. Seth made good his escape, taking Osiris's "third eye" (symbolic of kingship) with him. Meanwhile, Isis and Nephtys found their brother's body; while Isis wept and embraced the corpse, Osiris suddenly came to life long enough to impregnate her. The result of that union was the child god Horus, who, as soon as he was old enough, was asked by Isis to avenge his father's death.

Horus first appealed to the court of deities, accusing Seth of murdering his father. Because the court was slow to act, Horus then took the law into his own hands, killing Seth and recovering his father's third eye. As soon as Horus replaced the eye in his dead father's corpse, Osiris was resurrected. From then on, Osiris presided over the underworld as judge of the dead. He bequeathed his third eye to Horus, who wore it as the ruler and sun god of Egypt.

The erection of the pyramids and the process of mummification (embalming) are perhaps the best-known symbols of an Egyptian preoccupation with the afterlife.[7] The Egyptians perfected the technique of mummification to such a degree that a corpse could be preserved from decomposing almost indefinitely.

Retribution for the deeds of this life pervaded the thinking behind mummification. After death, so the Egyptians thought, everyone was fated to appear before the tribunal of Osiris. There, in the presence of Osiris and forty-two divine jurors, the newly dead were expected to confess to and exonerate themselves of various crimes, sins, and misdemeanours. To do that, the dead were buried with a guidebook or mortuary text, a collection of hymns, prayers, mythologies, and magical formulas gathered by scholars under the title *The Book of the Dead.*[8] The mortuary texts described the important experiences awaiting the deceased, along with a long list of "negative confessions," or protestations of guiltlessness, which the dead had to recite to certify themselves worthy of entering the land of Osiris.

After the plea, the Egyptians envisioned that the heart of the deceased person was weighed on a scale against an ostrich feather, the symbol of truth. If the heart overbalanced the scale, then retribution followed. One view held that the guilty were destroyed by the "Devouress," a terrifying and frightful creature. Another view was that retribution took the form of a fiery hell where the guilty writhed in nameless agony. If, however, the scales were balanced, the dead were permitted to enter the world of the blessed. There they were free to make use of the funerary articles stored in their tombs to speed their journey and ease their transition to the netherworld: these included chairs, beds, chariots, boats, kitchen utensils, combs, hairpins, cosmetics, gilded and silver objects of art, foodstuffs (such as jars of water, wine, grain, dates, cakes, portions of beef and fowl), and models of women and servants. Spells and incantations were provided to vivify the models of women and servants so they could be put to work as soon as their masters or mistresses arrived in the world of the blessed.

The theme of creation and the origin of all things reflect the rich variety of Egyptian mythologies, several of which are common to many religions. But unlike some religions, the mythology of Egypt does not provide a uniform pattern or an explanation for various phenomena.[9] On the contrary, several mutually exclusive – and sometimes contradictory – conceptions coexisted. For example, instead of a single account of the origin of things, several creation myths are found.

Creation is attributed to the creator god Atum (or Atum-Kheprer), who created air, moisture, earth, sky, and the deities and put his own vital force into the first creatures. But the Egyptians also viewed the god Ptah as the First Principle, taking precedence over other creator deities. Alternately, they saw the origin of everything as the work of Kheprer, the morning-sun god conceived of as a scarab beetle.

Attribution of creation to at least three divine agents is only one example of many apparent contradictions implicit in Egyptian mythology. Another contradiction involves the notion of the sky as being supported, variously on posts, on walls, and on a cow, by a goddess whose arms and feet touched the earth, or by a god. It is difficult, if not impossible, to establish which of those mythologies most appealed to the Egyptians. Possibly they represented regional or local variations on common themes or were beliefs held at different times.

A radical break from the established traditional Egyptian religion took place during the reign of the Pharaoh Amen-hotep IV (*ca.* 1380–1362 BCE), who moved his capital from Thebes to Tell-el-Amarna, changed his name to Akh-en-Aton (or Ikhnaton), and instituted the exclusive worship of Aton, the sun disk, as the creator and sustainer of all things.[10] Moreover, he ordered the priests to expunge the names and images of all deities other than Aton from all public records, monuments, and temples. He then created new centres throughout his empire, from Syria to Nubia, for the sole worship of Aton.

Because Akh-en-Aton was devoted to only one god, and because he identified that god as being exclusive and supreme (not merely the highest god among many), some scholars, though not all, have regarded him as the founder of monotheism (worship of one god). His monotheistic beliefs are best expressed in a hymn (composed *ca.* 1370 BCE) strikingly similar to the biblical hymn in Psalm 104 that praises God for his work of creation. The following parallel selections illustrate the generic similarities between the two compositions:

Psalm 104	Hymn to Aton
O Yhwh my God, thou art very great. Thou art clothed with honor . . . O Lord, how manifold are thy works! In wisdom has thou made them all; the earth is full of creatures. Thou didst set the earth on its foundations, so that it should never be shaken.	Thou dost appear beautiful on the horizon of heaven O living Aton . . . How manifold is that which thou has made, hidden from view! Thou sole god, there is no other like thee! Thou didst create the earth according to thy will, being alone: mankind, cattle, all flocks, everything on earth which walks with (its) feet, and what are on high, flying with their wings.

The similarity in spirit and wording of the Egyptian hymn to Psalm 104 often has been noted and discussed by scholars. The statement, "Thou sole god, there is no other like thee," is commonly cited by scholars as evidence of the monotheistic faith of Akh-en-Aton. Sigmund Freud offered in his book *Moses and Monotheism* (1939) the ingenious suggestion that Moses, who was raised in the Egyptian royal palace around that time, was influenced by Akh-en-Aton's monotheistic belief. Few scholars, however, take that proposal seriously.

Whatever links existed between Atonism and Mosaic religious traditions, the reforms instituted by Akh-en-Aton failed to survive his death. In fact, the new capital he founded was destroyed, his memory effaced, and the name of Aton obliterated from every public place. The succeeding pharaoh, Tut-ankh-Aton, changed his name to Tut-ankh-Amon (more popularly known today as King Tut) and yielded to the entreaties of his priests to return to traditional religious structures. Osiris, Isis, Horus, Amon-Re, and many other deities resumed their former status.

Sometime during these dramatic and decisive events Moses appeared. His biography is recorded in the Jewish scripture (Old Testament). So let us consider the traditional account as presented by biblical authors.

Traditional Account

The first and preeminent leader in the four books from Exodus to Deuteronomy is Moses.[11] The opening section of the book of Exodus relates how the descendants of Jacob's twelve sons find themselves as slaves in Egypt. And to make matters worse, the

Israelite population had grown to such a degree that the Egyptian government feared the Israelites would become too numerous to control. Consequently, the Egyptian pharaoh (king) ordered all male babies born to Israelite families to be killed. Moses, who was born during that period (perhaps the thirteenth century BCE), was hidden at home for three months, until the consequences of discovery prompted his mother to set her baby adrift in a waterproof basket in the rushes along the Nile River. There he was discovered by the pharaoh's daughter, who reared him in her palace as her adopted son.

Moses is the youngest of three children born to Jochebed (mother) and Amram (father), members of the Levites (Israel's priestly tribe). The older brother Aaron later became Israel's first High Priest, and his sister Miriam, who kept watch over the basket, approached Pharaoh's daughter and offered to find an Israelite woman to nurse the baby. The princess agreed, and Miriam took the baby to her mother, where Moses remained until he was weaned (perhaps 3–6 years).

As a young man, Moses witnessed a scene that became a turning point in his life: an Egyptian beating an Israelite. Moved by a sudden outburst of anger, he killed the Egyptian on the spot; soon after, Moses fled eastward and found refuge with Jethro, a Midianite priest (a Midianite was a member of a nomadic tribe that has long since disappeared). Eventually Moses married Zipporah, one of Jethro's daughters.

A second turning point occurred while Moses was herding Jethro's flock of sheep near Mount Horeb. There he experienced the presence of a divine being in a burning bush – an incident that not only changed his life but altered the destiny of his people in Egypt. The divinity charged Moses with bringing the Israelites out of the land of their enslavement and taking them to the "promised land" – the land of the Canaanites, where their ancestors had lived. Moses was assured by the divine presence, or God, that he would receive all the power necessary to persuade the pharaoh to let the Israelites go. Moses, however, comes up with all sorts of excuses and begs God to send anyone but him. In the end God tells Moses that his brother, Aaron, can assist him on this mission.

When Moses returned to Egypt, however, he found the pharaoh impervious to his pleas. Moses, directed by God, first threatened and then struck Egypt with nine terrible plagues in succession. Finally, the tenth plague, which struck and killed all the first-born sons of the Egyptians, including the pharaoh's, forced the pharaoh to let the Israelites go. Only the Israelite children were "passed over" (remained unharmed), and to this day the incident is commemorated as the "night of the Passover" or the Passover feast.

Moses then led the Israelites miraculously through the waters of the Red Sea (in Hebrew Reed Sea, whose exact location is disputed) and across the desert to the foot of Mount Horeb (sometimes referred to as Mount Sinai). This event, commonly known as the Exodus (from Greek meaning Going Out) played a basic role in the formation of the ancient Israelite people.

With Moses acting as the intermediary, a confrontation between God and the Israelites resulted in a solemn pact, commonly known as The Covenant. Tradition relates how Moses left the people at the foot of the mountain while he went up to communicate with God. Several days later, he returned with two stone tablets delivered to him by God and inscribed with the commandments of God, the familiar code known as the Ten Commandments.

The Ten Commandments

1. I am the Lord your God, who brought you out of the land of Egypt, out of the house of bondage. You shall have no other gods besides me.
2. You shall not make yourself a graven image, or any likeness of anything that is in heaven above, or that is in the earth beneath, or that is in the water under the earth; you shall not bow to them or serve them; for I the Lord your God am a jealous God, visiting the iniquity of the fathers upon the children to the third and fourth generation of those who hate me, but showing steadfast love to thousands of those who love me and keep my commandments.
3. You shall not take the name of the Lord your God in vain, for the Lord will not hold him guiltless who takes his name in vain.
4. Remember the Sabbath day, to keep it holy. Six days you shall labor, and do all your work; but the seventh day is a Sabbath to the Lord your God; in it you shall not do any work, you, or your son, or your daughter, your manservant, or your maidservant, or your cattle, or the sojourner who is within your gates; for in six days the Lord made heaven and earth, the sea, and all that is in them, and rested the seventh day, therefore the Lord blessed the Sabbath day and hallowed it.

5. Honour your father and your mother, that your days may be long in the land which the Lord your God gives you.
6. You shall not kill.
7. You shall not commit adultery.
8. You shall not steal.
9. You shall not bear false witness against your neighbour.
10. You shall not covet your neighbour's house; you shall not covet your neighbour's wife, or his manservant, or his maid-servant, or his ox, or his ass, or anything that is your neighbour's. (Exodus 20:1–17; cf. Deuteronomy 5:6–21)

Tradition maintains that the Israelites constructed a portable shrine, known as the Tabernacle of God, within which stood a box or chest containing the two stone tablets marked with the terms of The Covenant. As the Israelites continued their journey, Moses was able to commune with God in the interior of that portable shrine.

When Moses finally led the Israelites to the borders of Canaan, with the intention of invading it, they lost courage and rebelled against both Moses and God, bringing upon themselves years of wandering in the wilderness. This lasted for forty years, during which Moses had to cope with various waves of dissatisfaction and challenges to his leadership. Just before his death at the age of 120, Moses assembled the people and presented them with the Sinaitic legislation as well as his final blessing. Then he ascended Mount Nebo in Moab to view the "promised land" of Canaan, but died without entering the future home of the Israelites, because he disobeyed God at Marah by striking a rock to produce water, instead of only speaking to it as instructed by God. Thus, "God buried Moses in a valley in the land of Moab; but no one knows his burial place to this day" (Deuteronomy 34:6). Only under Joshua, Moses' successor, did the Israelites cross the River Jordan into the promised land of Canaan.

Principal Sources

Our knowledge about Moses' life and teachings derives from the Jewish scripture (known as the Old Testament by Christians). In its present form, the Jewish scripture contains twenty-four books and is divided into three main parts:

(1) The Law (*Torah*) containing five books
(2) The Prophets (*Nebi'im*) consisting of eight books
(3) The Writings (*Kethubim*) consisting of eleven books.

For Jews, the Torah is the most significant section of the Jewish scripture. Its authorship is traditionally ascribed to Moses. Biblical scholars have traced some of the basic ideas in the Torah to Moses, but the collection of writings, as it appears today, came into existence over a period of 600–700 years.[12] An enormous amount of study has been devoted to the identification of the authors, dates, and sequence of revisions of the Torah. The scholarly consensus is that there were at least four sets of editorial revisions (J=Yahweh, E=Elohist, D=Deuteronomic, P=Priestly), the last of which was undertaken by the priests during the exile in Babylon in the sixth century BCE. By 400 BCE, the five books of the Torah, as it appears today, attained the status of scripture.

The five books (Genesis, Exodus, Leviticus, Numbers, and Deuteronomy) contained in the Torah recounts the history of the Israelites from the days of their departure from Egypt, under the leadership of Moses, to the eve of their triumphant entry into the land of the Canaanites. Prefaced to this account are two other histories: the origin of the universe and humankind; and the stories and sagas of the individual patriarchs, Abraham, Isaac, Jacob and his twelve sons. Scattered among the accounts are various legal, social, and religious instructions or codes.

Thus, our only source of knowledge about an individual named Moses is the four books following Genesis, namely Exodus, Leviticus, Numbers and Deuteronomy. Ancient Near Eastern documents contain no references to him or to the role he played; and archaeological discoveries have not unearthed objects bearing his name or the wilderness journey. Therefore, the historicity of Moses, like the historicity of other biblical figures, depends on one's view of the Torah. To be sure, the themes emphasized in each book vary, but they all revolve around the life of Moses, from his birth in Exodus to his death in Deuteronomy.

Exodus relates three important events:

(1) escape of the Israelites from Egypt to Mount Sinai under the leadership of Moses (Exodus 1–18).
(2) making of a covenant and the receiving of the Law by Moses (Exodus 19–24).

(3) instructions for worship and the tent of meeting (Exodus 25–40).

There is also one poem – a song composed in honor of God (YHWH) – that biblical critics consider to be of the greatest antiquity (Exodus 15:1–18).

Leviticus contains legislation for the ritual of Israelite religion and regulations for the priests responsible for carrying out those instructions. The theme of the book centers around God's attribute of holiness and how Israel is to worship and maintain its relationship with the God of the Israelites. The book may be divided into four parts:

(1) laws about offerings and sacrifices (Leviticus 1–7).
(2) consecration of the Aaronite priests (Leviticus 8–10).
(3) laws about ritual cleanliness and uncleanliness (Leviticus 1–16).
(4) laws about holiness in life and worship (Leviticus 17–27).

The book of Leviticus contains no poetic composition. This is understandable, of course, because the book deals almost entirely with legislation for religious ritual performed by the Israelite priesthood.

Numbers contains an account of the Israelites who, during the nearly forty years they spent in the wilderness, were often afraid and discouraged, and who rebelled against Moses and his God who appointed him to lead them. The contents may be divided into four parts:

(1) military preparation to leave Mount Sinai (detailed in Numbers 1–10).
(2) travel from Mount Sinai to Moab with complaints and rebellions against Moses (Numbers 11–21).
(3) several incidents in Moab (Numbers 22–33).
(4) instructions before crossing the Jordan River (Numbers 34–36).

Also included in Numbers are several short verses (Numbers 21:15, 18, 27–30) and some oracular poems that were supposedly recited by a non-Israelite called Balaam ben Beor, intended to "curse" the Israelites (Numbers 23:7–10, 18–24; 24:3–9, 15–24).

Those poems are inserted in prose material that offers a humorous account (like a fable) of Balaam and his talking donkey.

Deuteronomy is organized as a series of discourses delivered by Moses to the Israelites in the land of Moab, just prior to their entrance and occupation of Canaan. The book's main theme is that the Israelites are to remember, love, and obey the commandments of God who loved, chose, and saved them. Five significant parts may be discerned:

(1) Moses' first discourse (Deuteronomy 1–4).
(2) Moses' second discourse (Deuteronomy 5–26).
(3) Instructions for entering Canaan (Deuteronomy 27–28).
(4) Renewal of covenant (Deuteronomy 29–30).
(5) Moses' last words, presenting Joshua as his successor, and Moses' death (Deuteronomy 31–34).

Two long poetic compositions (Deuteronomy 32:1–43; 33:1–29), both of which are said to have been recited by Moses before his death, conclude the book of Deuteronomy.

Thus the four books following Genesis describe the events and accomplishments that make up the life and teachings of Moses. And yet, our principal source of information, namely the "Torah of Moses," contains unresolved issues that are hotly debated among scholars. Let us consider this more closely.

The precise stages leading to the formation and recognition of the Jewish scripture are not easily discernible. Nevertheless, three concurrent stages can be distinguished in the literary process through which particular selections of Israelite writings came to be regarded as sacred. The first stage is identified with authorship and the creative task of writing. The second stage is associated with the editorial function: assembling materials, arranging them in sequence, clarifying, and developing consistency. The third stage marks the selection process and the inclusion of specific items within the final collection.

The first and most significant of these selections consisted of five books (Genesis, Exodus, Leviticus, Numbers, and Deuteronomy), collectively called Torah, a Hebrew word meaning Instruction or Law. Jewish tradition associated Moses with receiving divine law or instruction that are embodied in these books. The Torah was the result of a gradual and complicated process of selection and rejection.

The first indication of an authoritative book of the Law, or Torah, is found in 2 Kings 22:8–23:3, a passage that relates how the young King Josiah instigated (in *ca.* 621 BCE) a religious reform based on the "discovery" of the Law book. What this Law book contained is not clear, though scholars generally identify it as an early edition of Deuteronomy. References to the "Law Book" or "Law Book of Moses" appear also in Joshua 1:8, 8:31, 23:6 and 2 Kings 14:6. Another reference appears in Nehemiah 8–10, where it is said that Ezra the scribe read to the people of Jerusalem (either in 458 BCE or 398 BCE) from the "Law Book of Moses," which again became the basis of religious reform. Was Ezra's Law Book a copy of the earlier edition, or was it changed in the course of two centuries? Speculations by scholars range from the entire Torah to only portions of it.

Two other bodies of data provide further clues as to how the Torah was formalized. The first has to do with the intervention of Alexander the Great in Near Eastern affairs (334–323 BCE) and the subsequent influence of the dominating Hellenistic culture in his realm, especially Egypt. Pious Jews who lived in Egypt lost their understanding of Hebrew. This necessitated the translation of the Torah into Greek, which was probably done sometime between 300 and 200 BCE. The second relates to the Samaritan Jews, who separated from the rest of the Jewish community in Jerusalem. This event is one of the important incidents in Jewish history, but we do not know precisely when and why it happened. Judging from archaeological discoveries and literary studies, it seems that the final break occurred around the second century BCE, as a culmination of a long process of conflict between the Samaritan and Jerusalem communities. Today, the Samaritans possess a variant Hebrew text restricted only to the Torah, which has had a history quite separate from that of the formalized Hebrew text.

The Torah text of the Samaritans was written in a special script derived from the Old Hebrew script and copied over and over quite independently of the formalized Hebrew text. Moreover, the Samaritan text of the Torah, of which the most important surviving copy dates from the eleventh century CE, differs at several points from the standardized Hebrew text. It is estimated that these differences amount to some 6,000 instances, many of which are merely orthographic (i.e., variant ways of writing the same words), while others are trivial and do not affect the meaning of the text. However, what is significant is that in about 1,900 instances the Samaritan text agrees with the Septuagint (Greek translation of the Hebrew text), differing from the Hebrew text, and in other instances it corresponds to the Dead Sea scrolls. Furthermore, there are numerous intentional expansions and alterations reflecting the religious interests or tendencies of the Samaritans. Now, as the Samaritans possessed (and still possess) a different Hebrew version of the Torah, it seems reasonable to assume that the formalizing of the Torah was fixed before the breach between the two Jewish communities, about 400 BCE.

An Assessment

The collection of narratives about Moses in the books of Exodus to Deuteronomy are quite impressive; they demonstrate conclusively the role of Moses as a liberator, a leader, and a law-giver, from the moment of exodus from Egypt to the point of entry into Canaan. Nevertheless, biblical scholars disagree dramatically in their views of the historicity of the traditional narrative of Moses and of subsequent events. Some maintain that much of the account is a later pious fabrication. Others argue that all of the events occurred precisely as described. Still others insist that although much of the account was embellished in many ways by later editors, the memory of past experience is, in its major points, recorded correctly. Even the most sceptical critics, however, admit that *something* happened to give the Jewish people a new sense of destiny.

Although most scholars believe that a person named Moses existed, there is little agreement about how much can be known about Moses or the subsequent events ascribed to him. Anyone who has tried to study the available sources of information on Moses knows that the endeavor of sifting through the evidence to arrive at some tangible historical facts results only in the unpleasant feeling of uncertainty. In fact, the attempt to separate the historical from the unhistorical elements in the available sources has yielded few, if any, positive results regarding the figure of Moses. Critical investigation of the material has resulted in profound scholarly disagreements concerning his life and the part he played in the ancient Israelite people.

The scholarly disagreements revolve basically around the following issues:

- date and nature of the Israelites' entry into and departure from Egypt.
- circumstances surrounding Moses' birth and upbringing.
- relationship of the Midianites to Moses.
- content of the revelatory experience of Moses.
- historicity of the plagues sent upon Egypt.
- circumstances of the exodus and the route through the wilderness.
- location of, and the facts connected with, Sinai.
- relation between Moses and the Levites.
- incidents surrounding the challenge to Moses' leadership.
- authenticity of the account of the death of Moses.

Critical analysis on the role, status, and function of Moses is far more extensive than that listed above. Scholarly pursuits bent on solving specific problems related to the figure of Moses are too numerous to be mentioned here. Suffice it to say that this sort of critical operation violates the impressionistic elements in the narratives of a heroic leader.

The material on Moses contained in the four books from Exodus through Deuteronomy consists of an extended chronological sequence from Moses' birth to his death.[13] However, the selection of this biographical material includes only his genealogy and a few key events in his life: birth, adulthood, marriage, revelation, mission, and final moments. Moses' genealogy, particularly his relationship with the Levites, seems to be a remarkable attempt to synthesize a number of previously segmented narratives (Exodus 6:14–25; Numbers 26:57–60). The story of Moses' birth, especially the account of his being abandoned and found (Exodus 2:1–9), is borrowed from the story of Sargon, who was abandoned by his mother and set adrift in a reed basket on the river. He was rescued by Akki, the king's "drawer of water," and through the goddess Ishtar, Sargon eventually triumphed.

Moses' name (Hebrew *mosheh*) is of Egyptian derivation (e.g., Ah-Moses, Tut-Moses), but it is explained by the biblical narrator on the basis of a Hebrew etymology of assonance (i.e., Hebrew *masha* to draw out of the water; see Exodus 2:10). The events connected with Moses' youth and upbringing are, however, left unrecorded. Only one incident is mentioned that has to do with Moses' awareness of his roots. Moses is portrayed as disassociating himself from his royal upbringing by killing an Egyptian aggressor

Moses (Exodus 2)	Sargon
Now a man . . . married a woman, and the woman conceived and bore a son, and she hid him three months. When she could hide him no longer she made a basket of bulrushes and coated it with bitumen and pitch. Then she placed the child in it and put it among the reeds along the bank of the Nile. The Pharaoh's daughter went down to bathe at the river . . . she saw the basket among the reeds and sent her maid to bring it. When she opened it, she saw the child. He was crying, and she took pity on him. [Then the child's sister gets the mother to nurse the child for Pharaoh's daughter.] When the child grew up, she brought him to Pharaoh's daughter, and he became her son, and she named him Moses.	Sargon, the mighty king, king of Agade, am I. My mother was a changeling, my father I knew not. The brothers of my father loved the hills. My city is Azupiranu, which is situated on the banks of the Euphrates. My changeling mother conceived me, in secret she bore me. She set me in a basket of rushes, with bitumen she sealed my lid. She cast me into the river which rose not over me. The river bore me up and carried me to Akki, the drawer of water. Akki, the drawer of water lifted me out as he dipped his ewer. Akki, the drawer of water, took me as his son and reared me. Akki, the drawer of water, appointed me as his gardener. While I was a gardener, Ishtar granted me her love. And for four and . . . years I exercised kingship.

who was brutalizing a "Hebrew" slave. When the pharaoh learns of the deed, Moses has no choice but to escape to Midianite territory (Exodus 2:11–15).

The stories about his marriage, divine encounter, and mission, show the two differences of judgement regarding his biographic image. The reference to Moses' Cushite wife (Numbers 12:1) demonstrates one opinion, while the reference to Zipporah (meaning "birdie"; Exodus 2:21) demonstrates another. Incidentally, Zipporah, the wife of Moses, is said to have circumcised her son Gershom and thrown the child's bloody foreskin at Moses' feet (or genitals?) to appease God's threat to kill Moses (Exodus 4:24–26).

Again, one explanation of Moses' call or revelation includes the episode of Moses' weakness (Exodus 2:23–4:17), whereas another telling has expunged all signs of weaknesses (Exodus 6:2–13). One view presents the mission of Moses with signs of occasional despair and anger against God (Exodus 5:22–23, 17:4; Numbers 11:11–15), while another view presents him as second to none (Deuteronomy 34:10–12). As to the single account of the final moments of Moses, the statement that God shows him the promised land but bars his entrance (Deuteronomy 34:1–6) is clearly evidence of a sad ending.

The main purpose of presenting the biographical images of Moses is to reveal his unique relationship with God during the entire course of early history (Exodus 19:20, 24:15–18, 32:7–13, 33:9–34:30, etc.). Here is the classic reference: "YHWH spoke to Moses face to face, as a man speaks to his friend" (Exodus 33:11). This means that Moses was regarded by his biographer(s) as having realized in his own life direct contact with God. Are there any visible signs that indicate this extraordinary association between Moses and God? Yes, indeed!

Moses is presented neither as a world-renouncer, nor an ascetic, nor a monastic, nor an anchorite, nor a mystic. From the moment of his realization of God to the end of his life, Moses is depicted as the one who is empowered by God to perform "signs and wonders," that is, acts that are believed to violate the normal processes of life (e.g., Exodus 4:29–30, 7:1–11, 11:10, 14:21–29; Numbers 11:1–3, 20:7–11). In addition, he is shown as one who intercedes with God on behalf of the people (Exodus 32:7–14, 30–35; 33:12–17; 34:4–10; Numbers 11:1–3, 12:13–15, 16:20–22), acts as a judge on behalf of God (Exodus 18:13–27, Leviticus 24:10–23, Numbers 9:1–14; 15:32–36), receives the laws or commandments of God (Exodus 20:1–17; cf. Deuteronomy 5:6–21, Exodus 21–23, Leviticus 1–7, 11–27), and acts as a statesman representing the affairs of God (Numbers 1–2, 13, 20:14–31, 21:21–35). Later, in the book of Joshua, he is portrayed as the one who directs the distribution of the "inherited" land. All of these images were ultimately fused together to form an impressive biography, but the one that has stood the test of time is his role as the one who receives the laws or commandments of God.

These so-called commandments of Moses contain religious as well as social legislation (the traditional Jewish count is 613 *mitzvot*, or commandments) deriving from different authors and different periods. There are lengthy descriptions of how special days are to be observed and how rituals are to be performed, and details concerning festivals, offerings, and sacrifices; there are principles governing civil law, particularly in matters of marriage, family, inheritance, wages, debts, and slaves; and there are principles governing criminal law, such as murder, rape, adultery, sexual deviation, theft, assault, and liability. Penalties range from pronouncement of a curse to stoning and death. Other major elements of legislation deal with specific prohibitions: mistreating vulnerable classes (widows, orphans, or strangers), accepting bribes, perverting justice, and resorting to certain diviners, such as soothsayers, augurs, sorcerers, or mediums.

The collection of laws recorded in the books of Exodus through Deuteronomy seems to be the result of a long period of growth and development. The stages by which the legal corpus reached its present form correspond to different stages in the religious history of ancient Israel. Leviticus and Numbers contain the bulk of the cultic and ritual laws. They are presented as given to Moses by God at Mount Sinai after the construction of the sanctuary. While much of that law is undoubtedly ancient, there seems also to be supplementary material added at intervals thereafter. Similarly, Deuteronomy contains a set of civil and religious laws that are presented as deriving from the valedictory address of Moses – three discourses delivered on the last day of his life to an assembled audience in the wilderness. There are, however, many indications that suggest an accumulation of laws coming from various periods in Israelite history.

Another point to bear in mind is the close relationship between the biblical laws and their ancient Near Eastern counterparts, particularly Sumerian, Babylonian, Assyrian and Hittite laws. The connections between biblical and ancient Near Eastern law are undeniable, though the precise nature of such connections is difficult to determine. In many instances, biblical laws and ancient law codes are described in identical fashion (e.g., Exodus 23:1–3; Deuteronomy 19:16–20; Hammurabi Law I, 3, 4). In other instances, biblical laws and ancient Near Eastern laws are close but not identical (e.g., Exodus 21:2–11; Deuteronomy 15:12–18; Hammurabi Law 117). Another feature common to several of these Near Eastern and biblical codes is that they are introduced with a prologue and rounded off with an epilogue. The most obvious difference is that the biblical laws are presented within a continuous historical or narrative context. It is quite possible therefore that biblical authors utilized a common legal heritage, probably the Mesopotamian legal tradition.

Thus, the legal collections recorded in the books of Exodus, Leviticus, and Deuteronomy must have developed over a long period of time. In the end, Moses is presented as the one who receives the laws of God.

Just before the account of his death, the book of Deuteronomy records two poems recited by Moses (Deuteronomy 32:1–43; 33:1–29).[14] Unfortunately nothing is known about the author(s) or the precise dates of composition. What may be deduced, however, is that these poetic compositions were probably sung or recited long before they were committed to writing and placed appropriately among the prose works.

Because the biblical narratives on Moses occur in doublets, or show inconsistencies, it is difficult to know which material is historically authentic, if any. A few scholars consider Moses as the founder of Israelite religion, including the concept of monotheism. Their arguments are based on the following biblical passages:

- the answer Moses receives regarding God's name (Exodus 3:13);
- the worship of other gods by Moses' ancestors (Exodus 6:2–3);
- the giving of the law at Mount Sinai/Horeb as a covenant between God and the Israelites (Exodus 19–24); and
- the first two commandments mentioned in the Ten Commandments (Exodus 20:3–4).

Some scholars however doubt that Moses, as presented in the biblical books, is the founder of Israelite religion and of monotheism. And yet this position has been (and still is) the basis of Judaism. Consider the following statement by Rosalie David:

Moses founded the nation, impressed on it the teaching of monotheism and developed the covenant, previously between God and the individual patriarchs, into one between God and the nation as a whole. As the people's great lawgiver, he lay down the legal code which formed the basis of Judaism.[15]

The development of the Moses tradition among Jews, and later among Christians and Muslims, in the centuries that followed is a major topic that requires a separate volume. Suffice it to say that Jewish historians, rabbinic writers, as well as writings in the Christian scripture and the Holy Book of Islam, all mention Moses principally as leader, prophet, and lawgiver. Perhaps no other biblical passage mentions the role of Moses as explicitly as the passage considered to be his epithet:

And there arose not a prophet since in Israel like unto Moses, whom the Lord knew face to face. (Deuteronomy 34:10–12)

2

Jesus

In those days Jesus came from Nazareth of Galilee and was baptized by John in the [River] Jordan. And just as he [Jesus] was coming up out of the water, he saw the heavens opened and the spirit descending upon him like a dove. And a voice came from heaven, "You are my beloved son; with you I am well pleased."

(MARK 1:9–11)

The story of Jesus is the story of an individual whose religion took root within the framework of Judaism in Palestine but very quickly spread, first into Egypt, Persia, Arabia, Asia Minor (modern Turkey), later into Europe, and finally throughout the globe. Early in its history, the religious movement of Jesus embraced on equal terms many converts from Jewish, Greek, Roman, and other cultures. Almost from the very beginning its nature and scope was thought to be universal and not restricted to any particular group.

Hence, as it spread, the community of followers called Christian, absorbed and adopted a large number of religious elements and practices from Jewish, Persian, Greek, Roman and other ancient sources. Weekly assemblies for regular Sabbath services were a practice inherited from Judaism. The ideas of Satan (or the devil), angels and demons, heaven and hell, resurrection of the body, arrival of a Messiah, and other concepts were adopted from Zoroastrianism, the religion of the Persians. From the Greek culture, Christian scholars learned the art of logical argument and the expression of philosophical ideas. From Roman culture Christians borrowed the model of a centralized authority of law and order, and adapted it to fit an organized self-governing religious body, called the church.

Thus, the story of the life, death, and resurrection of Jesus has played a major role in the life of the Christian church. But first, who was Jesus, and what did he teach? Before answering those questions it is necessary to present a brief historical background on the religious world into which Jesus appeared.

Palestine: The Religious World of Jesus

The religious movement of Jesus emerged in Palestine (modern Israel) as a group of Judaism during the reign of the Roman Emperor Augustus Caesar, who ruled from 63 BCE to 14 CE.[1] The Romans had conquered Palestine in 63 BCE, and by the time of the birth of Jesus (*c.* 4 BCE), their empire had imposed a political unity on the lands bordering the Mediterranean that greatly facilitated the spread of various religions.

In its early stage, the Roman state was formed by a group of closely related tribes with similar cultures and common interests. In fact, it was conceived of as a great family, with the king exercising supreme control. All military, political, economic and religious power was vested in the king. According to tradition, seven kings ruled early Rome, though their power was limited by a council of advisors, called the Senate, and by an assembly of citizens. In 509 BCE the Romans rose against the ruling Etruscan king and established a republic.

During the republican period, the Romans gradually defeated and subjugated their rivals, expanding their territory until Rome became one of the most powerful nations on the Mediterranean littoral. In 149 BCE the Roman forces destroyed Carthage (in modern Tunisia), and in 146 BCE they completed their conquest of Greece by destroying Corinth. This victory paved the way for a Roman penetration of western Asia and an extension of their dominion over a large portion of the Middle East. Rome remained a republic until 27 BCE, when Augustus named himself emperor and vested himself with supreme authority. The establishment of an empire, however, did not at first radically alter forms of republican government; as time went on, however, the Senate lost its power and the emperor became an absolute monarch.

The expansion of Roman power during the republican period favoured Greek religious influences, especially the adoption of Greek deities; at this time many Roman gods became identified with Greek ones. Similarly, Greek education and philosophy penetrated Roman life and culture. During the Empire period, many Romans were attracted to ancient Middle Eastern religions, such as the worship of Cybele and Attis (Phrygian), Isis and Serapis (Egyptian), and Mithra (Persian).[2]

The first Middle Eastern mystery cult adopted by the Romans as a result of an oracular command was the worship of Cybele, the goddess of the Phrygians.[3] In 204 BCE, a black meteorite stone representing the foreign goddess was solemnly installed on the summit of the Palatine amid public cheering and incense fumes. Next, a temple was erected on the spot and an annual celebration was held from April 4 to 10 in commemoration of the arrival of the goddess, whom the Romans named the Great Mother Goddess of Idaea (or Ida). In a short time, however, the cult of Cybele encountered resistance from both the civil administration and the public, because of the orgiastic acts of its priests during the annual festival.

The annual festival of Cybele–Attis was held during the spring equinox and lasted four days, from March 22 to 25. On the first day, the trunk of a pine tree wreathed with violets and swathed with woollen cloth was carried ceremonially into the temple. Then, an effigy of the god Attis, Cybele's lover who was reputed to have died by emasculating himself under a pine tree, was fastened to the decorated tree trunk. On the second day, a procession of mourners followed the statue of the goddess Cybele through the streets. The mourners screamed, whirled, and leaped, and in their frenzy slashed themselves with knives and swords. On the third day, the bloody passion-drama reached its climax. Like Attis, the novitiates sacrificed their virility by emasculation, so they could share Attis's resurrection. The severed organs were offered on the altar of the goddess Cybele. The effigy was then removed and laid in a tomb, while the castrated initiates watched and fasted until the next morning. Early at dawn on the fourth day, the tomb was opened and the crowds of worshippers shouted in joy, because the god Attis was resurrected and the tomb was empty. The festival ended with a huge and joyous procession carrying the black meteorite stone (representing Cybele) to the river, where it was ceremonially bathed, after which it was returned to its sacred place in the temple.

In addition to that festival, some rituals were performed only by the emasculated initiates. Those ceremonies consisted of an initiatory rite, known as the *taurobolium*, and a sacramental meal. The *taurobolium* was a baptismal font in the form of a pit into which the newly inducted members descended, to stand under a grating that supported a sacred bull. The sacrificial bull was ceremonially slain on the grating so that its blood ran over the inductees below, who, by the ritual, were considered purified. The ritual of purification was followed by a sacramental meal, at which the inductees shared a sense of oneness or unity as they ate from a common drum and drank from a common cymbal.

The similarity between some aspects of the rites associated with Cybele–Attis and the Christian celebration of the resurrection of Jesus is striking. Two coincidences are noteworthy: first, the site of Cybele's temple is where the basilica of St. Peter's stands today; second, the annual spring celebration of the death, burial, resurrection, and discovery of an empty tomb is a feature both of the ancient rites of Cybele–Attis and the annual spring celebration of Easter, or *Pascha*, which commemorates the death, burial, resurrection, and discovery of the empty tomb of Jesus.

The worship of the Egyptian goddess Isis was introduced to Rome around the second century BCE, but long before that the popularity of her cult had spread far and wide.[4] Her statues and temples adorned Syria around the seventh century BCE, and three centuries later a great temple was built for Isis at the foot of the Acropolis in Greece. Soon every Greek city and village had a temple and a statue of Isis. The statue of Isis, which represented the Mother Goddess with her suckling infant son, Horus, became an object of veneration in the Greco-Roman world. Some scholars are of the opinion that Christian images and statues of the Madonna and child (Mary and the infant Jesus) resemble those of Isis and her son.

The goddess Isis was regarded as the symbol of maternal love, protection, creative life, and chastity, and she was regarded as the queen of heaven. Because she encompassed such virtues, her cult attracted a large number of followers. Two festivals, one in spring and the other in autumn, were celebrated in her honor. The spring festival coincided with the Egyptian harvest, while the autumn celebration consisted of a four-day dramatic festival. On the first day of the autumn festival, actors impersonated several Egyptian deities, including Isis and Horus, who wept, wailed, and searched for the body of Osiris. On the next two days, portions of the body of Osiris were found, reconstituted, and resurrected by Isis. On the fourth day, a great rejoicing took place, because Osiris had been resurrected and become immortal. Devotees of Isis could celebrate her assurance of life after death and immortality by drinking the milk of Isis from a chalice in the shape of a woman's breast. Those who put their trust in Isis did so with the conviction that she would intercede on their behalf with Osiris when they appeared before his throne of judgment and that Osiris would in no way deny immortality to those for whom Isis interceded.

The Egyptian god Serapis also was closely associated with the mythology surrounding Osiris. The name was a Hellenized combination of Osiris and Apis, the Egyptian bull god. His cult originated in Alexandria, Egypt, and from the beginning it was identified with Osiris, the god who ruled the dead and shared immortality with them. Its adoption by the Romans began around the second century BCE, although a century later the Roman Senate took strict measures to stop its diffusion. Nevertheless, the worship of Serapis, like the cult of Isis, invaded Italy and every imperial province. Not until five centuries after they had been adopted by the Romans were the cults of Isis and Serapis finally suppressed. In 390 CE the Christian Patriarch Theophilus, with the aid of the Roman Emperor Theodosius, consigned the temple of Serapis in Alexandria to the flames. Between the reigns of the emperors Theodosius and Justinian, an interval of about two hundred years, the worship of Isis, Serapis, Cybele, Attis, and all other Greek, Roman, and foreign deities was extirpated in favour of Christianity.

Of all the foreign religions adopted by the Romans, the worship of the Persian (Iranian) god Mithra became the most popular and widespread.[5] Introduced into the Roman Empire in the first century BCE, Mithraism spread so rapidly that in a very short time hundreds of Mithraeums (temples) had been established from India to Scotland through the agency of zealous Mithraic proselytes, who communicated their convictions with missionary fervor along the ancient trade routes of Africa, Italy, Germany, Spain, France, and Britain. Roman emperors, senators, soldiers, and civil servants were among the most ardent supporters of Mithra. That was not surprising, because Mithra was the invincible god of war, the protector of stable government, and the upholder of social justice and brotherhood.

Mithra was an ancient Indo-Aryan god that appeared in the religion and mythologies of the ancient Persians (Iranians) and the Indians. As the lord of heavenly light, he was identified with the sun, but he also was the god of cattle, agriculture, war, and truth. In addition, Mithra was one of the judges who welcomed the souls of humans after death and, as the god of immortality, he conferred everlasting life on his faithful followers. No documents or scriptures are extant on Mithra, but scholars have been able to analyze the cult based on fragmentary references, inscriptions, bas-reliefs, and sculptures. On the basis of all that material, scholars have reconstructed the following story about Mithra.

According to the story, the god Mithra was born miraculously in a cave on December 25. The event was witnessed only by some shepherds who came with their gifts to worship the newborn god. From infancy, Mithra's mission was to become master of the earth. To that end he made the sun subject to his will and consequently was identified with it. Next, he considered it his duty to sacrifice a bull, the pristine creation of the Persian god Ahura Mazda (see chapter on Zoroaster). That sacrifice was imperative, because the Persians believed that the soul of the bull was the generative source of all celestial elements, and its body the source of human life and all life on earth: all useful herbs from its carcass; wheat from its spinal marrow; all useful animals from its semen; and grapes, which produced the sacramental wine consumed during Mithraic rituals, from its blood. Mithra, therefore, was identified with the slain bull as the creator of all beneficent creatures and herbage. Above all, Mithra was the savior god who protected his devotees in this world and granted them salvation in the next.

Mithraic congregations consisted only of male communicants, who gathered in small numbers of perhaps one hundred or so in underground or subterranean meeting places, because Mithra was born in a cave. Members passed through seven orders or degrees, including an initiation ritual, in which the outline of a cross was branded on their foreheads. Newly inducted members, like their counterparts in Cybelian *tauroboliums*, stood under a grating on which a sacred bull was ceremonially slain, soaking them in the bull's blood. They also took an oath never to reveal the secrets of the order or the mysteries of Mithra. Induction into higher orders involved purification; baptism by fire in a ceremony that required postulants to submit to a sign marked on their foreheads with a hot iron; and the sacraments of bread and wine, representing mystical union with the god Mithra.

Sunday was holy to the followers of Mithra, because it glorified the sun god, Mithra. December 25 was hallowed because it was the birthday of Mithra, and devotees kept a vigil on the preceding night.

The striking parallels between Mithraism and Christianity hardly need to be pointed out. Both taught that their founders were mediator savior gods, through whom the salvation of human beings was possible and through whom the world would be judged. Both taught the doctrines of heaven and hell, the last judgment, and the immortality of the soul; that the forces of good and evil were in a state of perpetual conflict; and that self-control and abstinence were requisites to acceptance. Both offered the sacraments of baptism and communion and observed each Sunday and December 25 as holy days.

For five centuries followers of Mithraism enjoyed complete freedom of worship throughout the Roman Empire. However, the accession of Emperor Constantine in 311 CE and his encouragement and support of Christianity drastically changed that situation. The hatred that Christians exhibited toward Mithraism and the terrible persecution they perpetrated against its adherents ultimately destroyed it. The most extreme measures against Mithraism came during the reign of Emperor Theodosius in the fourth century, when the once widespread mystery cult of Mithra was completely extirpated by the followers of Christianity.

One of the main features and last manifestations of Roman religion was the deification of the emperors, which took hold in the first century CE, at the end of the Republican Period and the beginning of the Empire.[6] At that time, many native Roman gods were losing popularity and their temples were being deserted. Patriotic statesmen and influential poets started to endow emperors with divine qualities, elevating them beside the old Roman gods as objects of worship. Thus, upon their deaths, if not during their lives, the emperors were raised to the status of Roman deities.

Some scholars consider the deification of the emperors to have been rooted in the ancient Roman view of the quality or attribute that Romans identified as *genius* (a family or ancestral spirit, derived from the *numen* Genius) that was bequeathed or transmuted from the dead as a divine force to the clan. (A clan is a social unit smaller than a tribe but larger than a family.) Other scholars speculate that the practice was borrowed from Egyptian pharaoh worship. Whatever its ultimate origins, emperor worship was initiated with Julius Caesar, when the Senate declared him a god in 44 BCE, before his death. Emperor Augustus, the adopted son and successor of Julius Caesar, further honored his father with a temple erected and dedicated in his name (Divus Julius). Henceforth, it became customary to add the divine epithet *divus* to the emperor's name after his death.

Emperor Augustus himself permitted the erection of shrines in which his *genius* was worshipped. In fact, paying reverence to the emperor's *genius* (and sometimes to the emperor himself) became a sign of loyalty to the Roman Imperium. In due time, the aura of divinity was accorded to every emperor as a matter of course during his lifetime. Emperors Nero, Caligula, Domitian, and Trajan were among those who demanded the status of god during their lifetime. Emperor Nero is said to have enjoyed being equated with Apollo.

As an expression of patriotism, emperor worship perhaps attained a degree of success, but it failed as a unifying element to give various religious faiths one inclusive meaning or purpose as a focus for Roman citizens and society.

Religiously, the Roman Empire was pluralistic. Greek and Roman religions were tolerated from the earliest times, and in the first century BCE emperor worship was encouraged, chiefly as a means of promoting loyalty to the empire. Mystery cults, largely of Middle Eastern origin, were popular and widespread. Because the temper of the age was syncretistic, the mystery religions borrowed extensively from one another, and over time they came to share a number of common attributes. Of most importance, every cult centered on a "savior god" who had died and been resurrected. Adherents attained immortality by sharing symbolically in the death and resurrection of the savior god, whether he was called Mithra, Osiris, Adonis, Attis, Orpheus, or Dionysus.

Ultimately the religion of the "savior god" Jesus triumphed over all the others, but that must have seemed an unlikely outcome of events in the early days of Roman tolerance. Not only were many religions tolerated, but so were many sectarian and nonconforming groups within religions.

In Judaism, for instance, the Pharisees, who acted as the representatives of Jewish beliefs and practices, were concerned mainly with preserving the Jewish faith from compromises with Hellenism. The Sadducees, heavily represented in the wealthy elements of the population, controlled the central Temple in Jerusalem. The Zealots were fanatic patriots who refused any compromise with Rome and opposed all attempts to make Palestine subservient to Roman powers. Their revolt in 66–70 CE, which the Romans ruthlessly crushed, resulted in the burning of the Temple in Jerusalem and the dispersion of the Jews. The Essenes, a small communal group that lived in the vicinity of Qumran, by the Dead Sea, opposed violence, lived by strict monastic rules, and patiently awaited the coming of the messiah (anointed one of God), who would deliver the Jews from foreign oppression. A number of biblical scholars think that Jesus belonged to that group.[7]

The Jews had held hope of the coming of a messiah (as an ideal "savior king") during their captivity in Egypt, long before they returned to Israel. Saul and David, the first two kings of Israel, were initiated into their royal office by anointing. Later, generations that faced misfortune and destruction looked back to David as the ideal king and longed for a scion (son) of David who would deliver them from their oppressors and restore their ancient glory. During the exilic period, that longing took the form of a messianic hope that God would send his anointed one (messiah) to deliver his people from their enemies. Under the Roman rule, particularly in the first and second centuries CE, messianic hope became so strong among the Jews that many self-proclaimed messiahs appeared. Sometime during these dramatic and decisive events Jesus appeared. But who was Jesus? When and where was he born? What did he teach?

Traditional Account

The basic information concerning the life and teachings of Jesus is recorded in the four Gospels (sacred texts of Christianity called New Testament). Jesus left no written records. Sources of information that have survived are restricted primarily to the four Gospels which do not read like verbatim reports of Jesus' words. Rather, the contents of the Gospels suggest that each writer used the material according to his own purposes and prejudices. That is not to imply that the Gospel writers distorted the message of Jesus, merely that what they wrote is likely to have been affected by their own perspectives as members of a community of early Christian believers.

The date and place of Jesus' birth cannot be determined with certainty. According to the Gospel of Matthew, Jesus was born in Bethlehem in the days of King Herod, who died in 4 BCE. The Gospel of Luke, however, suggests two other dates: first, that Jesus was born in Bethlehem when Quirinius was governor of Syria, 6–9 CE; second, that Jesus was baptized at age thirty in the fifteenth year of the reign of Emperor Tiberius (26 or 27 CE), suggesting 4–3 BCE as the date of Jesus' birth.

It was not until the sixth century CE that a Christian monk divided history into BC ("Before Christ") and AD (*Anno Domini*, "year of our Lord"), to relate the birth of Jesus to the ancient Roman calendar. Whether or not that monk's calculation was correct, the beginning of the Christian era is assumed to date from the birth of Jesus. This reckoning has been accepted by the church and hallowed by long use.

Regarding the place of Jesus' birth, Gospel writers vacillate between Bethlehem in Judea (Matthew 2:1) and Nazareth in Galilee (Luke 1:26–27, 57; John 1:45), locations some 200 miles apart. The early Christians (and hence the Gospel writers) may have been influenced by the desire to make Jesus a descendant of King David from Bethlehem and thus link him to Old Testament prophecies concerning the Messiah. But because all of the Gospel writers agree that the family of Jesus lived in Nazareth, scholars have been inclined to attach greater credibility to the theory that the latter was Jesus' birthplace.

Little is known about the childhood and youth of Jesus. Mark and John make no mention at all of Jesus' virgin birth, childhood, or youth. On the other hand, Matthew and Luke declare that Jesus was born from the Virgin Mary and that supernatural events occurred at the time of his birth (Matthew 1:18–25; Luke 1:26–45). Luke goes on to describe Jesus' circumcision rite when he was eight days old and his learned conversation with the Jewish rabbis in the Temple at Jerusalem when he was twelve (Luke 2:42–50). Mark and Matthew imply that Jesus' trade, like that of Joseph, Mary's husband, was carpentry and that he had four brothers and a number of sisters (Mark 3:31; 6:3; Matthew 12:46; 13:55–56). Almost nothing else is known of his early years.

The Gospels relate that when Jesus was about thirty years old, a stern Jewish ascetic, John the Baptist, appeared in Galilee and announced the coming judgment of God in the person of a messiah, who would deliver the Jews from Roman rule. Standing by the River Jordan, he proclaimed, "Repent, for the kingdom of heaven is coming" (Matthew 3:2). Jesus was among those who were baptized in the river by John the Baptist.

That incident may have marked the turning point in Jesus' life. He at once withdrew to the wilderness beyond the Jordan, before finally deciding on his future career. What actually happened during his forty days in the wilderness is a mystery. Mark states that Jesus lived there with the wild beasts and that angels ministered to him (Mark 1:13). Matthew and Luke say that Satan appeared in person and challenged Jesus with three temptations. First, to prove his divinity, Jesus was challenged to convert the stones to bread. He declined, saying, "One does not live by bread alone." Second, Satan invited Jesus to throw himself from the top of the Temple in Jerusalem to land unharmed. Again, he declined, saying, "Do not put the Lord your God to the test." Finally, Jesus was offered control of the entire world if he would bow down and worship Satan. Jesus replied, "Go away Satan!" an injunction that Satan followed without further urging (Matthew 4:3–11; Luke 3:1–13).

As soon as Jesus came out of the wilderness he returned to Galilee to find that John the Baptist had been arrested and imprisoned. Jesus felt that the time had arrived for him to assume his role. He now repeated John's message: "Repent, for the kingdom of heaven is coming!" (Matthew 4:17).

According to the Gospels, Jesus attracted a group of twelve disciples, who constantly travelled with him from place to place proclaiming the "good news." Some of his disciples were fishermen, others were artisans, and one was a tax collector – a profession widely despised, because it was identified with graft and subservience to Rome. At first, Jesus spoke in Jewish synagogues, but when the crowds grew too large, he resorted to open places.

The events recorded in the Gospels establish Jesus' authoritative personality, his keen interest in and compassion for people, and his reputation for healing. His forceful speeches and imaginative use of parables attracted large crowds. Relating easily to people of all types, including prostitutes and social outcasts, he apparently disdained social barriers and prejudices.

He also made enemies, chiefly by challenging time-honored assumptions. He ignored a number of Jewish traditions, such as Sabbath restrictions and ritual cleanliness, and scorned those who in his view had substituted social and ceremonial practices for inward morality. Sternly rebuking those who professed to be religious but were insincere and hypocritical, he offended Jewish scribes and leaders by openly attacking them for their views and behavior regarding authority, the Torah, divorce, taxes, and resurrection. His reputation varied according to the viewpoints of three disparate groups: to the scribes, he was an imposter and a deceiver; to much of the public, he was a prophet; and to his disciples, he was the Son of God (Matthew 14:33).

Jesus' mission lasted only a year or two before he, like John the Baptist, was arrested. The reasons for his trial and execution, as implied in the Gospels, are puzzling and contradictory. The only fact that is clearly and unambiguously recorded is that Jesus met his death on the cross, just like any other convicted rebel or criminal under the Roman administration.

The events that followed the death of Jesus were of greater importance to early Christians than were the events that preceded it. The Gospels record three phenomenal incidents. First, Jesus was resurrected three days after his crucifixion, and he subsequently appeared to many of his followers on numerous occasions. Second, forty days after his resurrection he was lifted up to heaven in the presence of a group of people who heard a voice saying,

> Men of Galilee, why do you stand looking into heaven? This Jesus, who was taken up from you into heaven, will come in the same way as you saw him go into heaven. (Acts 1:10–11)

Third, ten days after the ascent of Jesus – on the day of the Jewish festival of Shavuot – a group of Jesus' followers spoke in "strange" languages and claimed to have been filled with the Holy Spirit.

All of those events laid the groundwork for various new insights among the followers of Jesus, in particular, the attribution to him of "godhood" and the proclamation of him as the "Son of God." That Christian insight steadily spread to various parts of the Roman Empire and the Persian Empire. Little did the early Christians realize that their message was to affect humanity so deeply. Based on the few years of association with Jesus, the disciples went about spreading the stories of Jesus – what he did and what he taught.

The Gospel of John states that if everything Jesus did and taught were to be recorded, then "the world itself could not contain the books that would be written" (John 21:25), suggesting that Jesus said much more than was recorded in the Gospels. Consequently, identifying precisely what Jesus taught is as difficult as establishing his identity.

Principal Sources

As has been pointed out, Jesus left no writing of his own; so scholars have had to rely on three other sources of information about his life and teachings. The four Gospels in the New Testament, namely, Matthew, Mark, Luke, and John, are the most important source of information. All four Gospel writers record the life of Jesus, but each starts with a different approach and relates the story from a different perspective. The four Gospels, therefore, are the primary source of information concerning Jesus and his teaching.

Next are the writings of Paul, collected in the New Testament, although he had no close relationship with Jesus. Finally, a few references are made to Jesus by classical writers of the first and second centuries CE. What they say about Jesus, however, does little more than establish his historical existence.

Apparently, many writings and collection of stories circulated widely during the first four to five hundred years of the history of the Christian church. Eventually, a number of writings (twenty-seven in total) were selected and assembled to form the New Testament (in *c.* 397 CE).

First in order are the four Gospels (Matthew, Mark, Luke, and John), which record the life and teachings of Jesus. They are followed by the book known as the Acts of Apostles, chronicling the history of the early Christian missionaries. Succeeding the Acts is a number of Epistles – letters written by various disciples (most notably Paul) either to individuals or to Christian communities. The last book, Revelation, is a visionary account of the final triumph of God. The entire New Testament was written in Hellenistic Greek, the common language in the eastern Roman Empire (outside Palestine and the neighboring countries).

The four Gospels and the writings of Paul are not merely accumulations of historical facts. Rather, they are documents of faith and as such are primarily concerned with the theological implications of the life and teachings of Jesus. Biblical scholars generally assume that after the death of Jesus some of his disciples recorded his sayings before they were forgotten. [8] That group of documents is called "Q" (from the German word *Quelle*, meaning "source"). It is further assumed that the Q documents, although on the whole authentic, were colored by presuppositions and included sayings mistakenly ascribed to Jesus. Furthermore, the Gospel writers – particularly Matthew and Luke – are assumed to have used a great deal of material from the Q documents.

In addition, the first three Gospels (Matthew, Mark, and Luke) are designated "Synoptic" by biblical scholars to account for the extensive and complex combination of similarities and differences within them, as distinguished from the fourth Gospel (John). The distinction between the perspectives of the Synoptic Gospels and the Gospel of John concerns the amount of material involved, the order of events, style, content, and method of the teachings of Jesus, and the religious perspective of the writers. The first three Gospels can be grouped together as a unit because they share common characteristics. Yet when they are arranged in the parallel columns of synopsis, a puzzling combination of similarities and differences emerges. Suffice it to say that the continued discussion by scholars over many details indicates that they are trying to uncover the preliterary formation of the Gospels. Thus two conclusions remain undisputed: Jesus himself wrote nothing, and the content of the four Gospels suggests or implies two sources – one, a record of sayings ascribed to Jesus, and the other, contemporary opinion reflecting the understanding of early Christians.

In its earliest form, Christian literature consisted of letters, or epistles. The epistles of Paul are probably the earliest writings in the New Testament. Some time during the first century, a number of Paul's letters circulated among Christians. The four Gospels of the New Testament also appeared in the same century. However, there seemed to be no attempt on the part of the early Christian community to regard those writings as scripture. During the second century, a flood of gospels and other literature forced Christians to make selections in their estimation of an authoritative Christian literature. The earliest exact reference to the current collection of books in the New Testament appeared in 367 in a letter of Athanasius, bishop of Alexandria. A complete listing of the books of the Old and New Testaments was provided at a council held in Rome in 382. Thus, the Christian Bible took its final shape by the late fourth century.

An Assessment

Biblical scholars have carefully examined the Gospels as primary material in an attempt to discover the basic message of Jesus. Based on current knowledge and methodology, a number of biblical scholars recognize that the Gospels contain both reliable historical memories of the words and deeds of Jesus as well as information that is not historical but that has been attributed to Jesus by later Christians.[9] Although scholars differ widely over the basic message of Jesus, most assert that Jesus' teaching encompasses one or more of the following concepts: the Fatherhood of God, the Kingdom of God, God's love of humankind, and God's universal plan of salvation. The crucial question underlying those concepts is whether Jesus considered himself God incarnate or his followers endowed him with that status after his death. The question remains unresolved, because the Gospels present clear evidence justifying both views. Although it is impossible to examine in a few pages all of those views, an attempt is made here to consider the basic concepts and teachings of Jesus, as recorded in the Gospels.

From the time of his baptism by John the Baptist to the end of his short life, the reality of God occupied the central place in the thoughts of Jesus. His own intimate relationship with God deeply impressed his disciples, as he strongly emphasized the Fatherhood of God. He regarded every human being as more than just a creature or servant of God – each individual was a child of God.

When his final hours of life on this earth were approaching, Jesus celebrated the Jewish annual Passover feast with his disciples for the last time and spoke to them after what has become known as the Last Supper. The Gospels give us a vivid account of what Jesus spoke about. It is there that Jesus reveals not only his deep relationship and intimacy with the Father, but how that relationship signifies to him complete union or oneness with the Father (John 14: 7, 9, 11, 28–31; 17:1). Touched by Jesus' insight and prayer, the disciples followed him to the garden of Gethsemane. Deeply distressed and full of sorrow, Jesus fell to the ground and earnestly prayed once again (Mark 14:32–36). When finally Jesus was crucified situated between two criminals, his words once again revealed his close relationship to God (Luke 23:34). And his last words on the cross were, "Father, into thy hands I commit my spirit" (Luke 23:46).

That personal closeness to the Father was the characteristic feature of Jesus' teaching. In fact, he taught that God was everyone's Father, and that every person could communicate directly and intimately with him, regardless of place or time. "Beware of practicing your piety before men in order to be seen by them," said Jesus, "For then you will have no reward from your Father who is in heaven" (Matthew 6:1).

Jesus not only made all who heard him distinctly aware of their relationship to God but directed their attention to the coming Kingdom of God, which he referred to as the "Kingdom of Heaven" (see Matthew 13 and 18–21 for parables of the Kingdom). "The Kingdom of Heaven may be compared to . . ." was the way Jesus began much of his teaching about God's Kingdom. His analogies regarding the Kingdom of Heaven covered a wide range of everyday activities that everyone could understand.

Whatever else Jesus may have implied by teaching about the Kingdom of Heaven, this much is certain: he urged everyone to seek primarily the Kingdom of God and His righteousness. He assured his hearers that God as a Father cared for every individual; no person was unworthy of receiving the Father's grace. Moreover, no person was to be excluded from the Kingdom of Heaven, for it was accessible to all who asked (Matthew 7:7–8).

A person's relationship to God is reasonably clear from the teachings of Jesus. What is less clear is how Jesus saw himself in relationship to God. Did he think of himself as a child or son of God in the same sense as he taught that everyone was a child or son of God? Or did he consider himself to be the "Son of God" in a special sense? Did he regard himself as the Messiah (the Lord's anointed), or was it his disciples who later thought of him as the Messiah?

Obviously those questions have represented, and still represent, the knottiest issues of interpretation in the history of Christianity. And perhaps such crucial problems never can be finally answered. Nevertheless, one thing is beyond doubt: Jesus knew that he was "sent" to proclaim the Kingdom of Heaven and the Fatherhood of God (Luke 4:16–21, 43). Hence, he proclaimed that the Father's love for a person is so great and boundless that it is not governed by a person's goodness or wickedness. God manifests his love and mercy to all human beings – both good and bad – without regard to need or merit.

Jesus taught that the two concepts, the Fatherhood of God and the union of humankind, are inseparable. An individual who experiences an intimate fellowship with God the Father must of necessity love humankind. In fact, anyone who does not love human beings can know nothing about God, let alone be associated with Him. To love the individual who is unjust, cruel, deceitful, ugly, and unlovable, and to love the murderer, the social outcast, and one's enemy as much as the good and the lovable, is to love God. To feed the hungry, to clothe the naked, to welcome the stranger, to cheer the sick, to visit the imprisoned – in short, to love and serve humanity is to love and serve the Father (Matthew 25:24–46).

That teaching so impressed the minds of many that an expert in Judaic Law (the Torah) once asked Jesus to explain what he meant by "loving one's neighbor as oneself" (Luke 10:29–37). Jesus replied by telling the story of a man who was robbed, beaten, stripped, and left to die on the road. A priest and a teacher who happened to pass that way saw the man but ignored him and travelled on. A Samaritan (one of the Jewish groups regarded as an enemy by traditional Jews at that time) who was the next traveller to pass, pitied the man, stopped, helped him, and took care of all his needs.

> "Which of these three," said Jesus, "do you think, proved neighbor
> to the man who fell among the robbers?"
> The one who showed mercy to him.
> "Then go and d\o likewise," said Jesus.

On another occasion, Jesus taught his disciples the future joy of participation in the Kingdom of God, rather than rewards for this earthly life. This is clearly apparent in the familiar passage "The Beatitudes of the Sermon on the Mount" (Matthew 5:3–12; cf. Luke 6:20:23).

The principles of love and mercy for Jesus far outweighed any others. There was no question in his mind that the highest goal in life, the most valuable element in living, was to demonstrate God's nature: love, mercy, and compassion to one and all. One question, however, still eludes us. What was Jesus' own view about human nature? Did he agree that one was "born in sin" and inherently evil? Is evil part of one's makeup, such as one's lungs or the hair on one's head?

Two Gospel writers, Luke and John, have nothing to say about "original sin." The other two Gospel writers, Matthew (15:1–20) and Mark (7:1–23), however, record a discussion among Jesus and certain Jewish religious authorities who questioned him regarding the Tradition of the Elders.

> "Why do your disciples transgress the Tradition of the Elders, and
> eat with hands defiled [ritually unwashed]?" they asked.
> "And why do you transgress the commandment of God for the sake
> of your Tradition?" Jesus asked.

Then Jesus turned to all who were present there and said,

> Hear me, all of you, and understand: not what goes into the mouth
> defiles a man, but what comes out of the mouth, this defiles a man.

When his disciples showed by their questions that they did not understand what he was talking about, Jesus went on to say,

> Do you not see that whatever goes into a man from outside cannot defile him, since it enters not in his heart but his stomach, and so passes on? What comes out of a man is what defiles a man. For from within, out of the heart of man, come evil thoughts, fornication, theft, murder, adultery, coveting, wickedness, deceit, licentiousness, envy, slander, pride, foolishness. All these evil things come from within, and they defile a man." (Matthew 15:1–20)

Thus, Jesus declared that sin lies deep in the heart of a human being. What lies in the heart – the hidden attitudes and motives – rather than outward actions should be judged. But his statement offers no explanation of the nature of sin. Nor does he mention anything about original sin. It may be that his idea of the nature of sin was similar to one of the then current Judaic concepts, but certainly he shows no interest in defining sin or its origin in the abstract sense.

3
Muhammad

And he heard a voice saying to him: "Muhammad, you are God's messenger." Terrified and overwhelmed by this divine apparition, Muhammad fell prostrate. The voice commanded, "Recite!" Then Muhammad asked in terror: "What shall I recite?" And the answer came: "Recite   in the name of your Lord who created!
Created man from clots of blood! Recite   for your Lord is most beneficent . . . .who has taught man that which he knew not."
(QURAN, SURA 96:1–4)

Islam was established in Arabia in the seventh century as a result of the message of the Prophet Muhammad.[1] It developed with astonishing speed into a great cohesive civilization, extending all the way from the Atlantic Ocean to the borders of China. Today, it is one of the world's most widely diffused religions. More than half of the total Muslim population is found in the East: China, south-eastern Asia, and the Indian peninsula, including, Burma, and Sri Lanka. The remaining Muslims are dispersed across eastern Europe (including Turkey), the Balkan nations, Russia, the Middle East (including the Arab world), and Africa. Small groups are also found in various Western countries, including, Germany, France, Britain, Canada, and the Americas. The birthplace of this compelling new faith was Arabia, then a semi-nomadic and semi-urban civilization. Two extreme views regarding the origin of Islam are worth noting.

The origin of Islam lies either in the sixth century CE in Arabia or at the beginning of time, at creation, depending upon the point of view one wishes to take. From the Muslim perspective, the story of Islam starts not with Muhammad, but shares a common tradition with Judaism and a common biblical origin when God created the world and the first man, Adam. The descendants of Adam are traced to Noah, who had a son named Shem. The descendants of

Shem are then traced to Abraham and his wife Sarah and her handmaid Hagar. At this point, two familiar stories about Abraham provide the cornerstones of the Islamic religion. The first, Abraham's attempted sacrifice of his son Isaac, demonstrates the submission of Abraham in the supreme test: hence the term "Islam" (Arabic, meaning "submission" "peace"). The second, concerning Ishmael's banishment, gave rise to the belief that Ishmael (the son of Abraham and Hagar) went to Mecca and that eventually from his descendants the prophet Muhammad emerged in the sixth century CE.

Another point of view is that the Islamic religion began with its founder Muhammad, who was born in Mecca, in Arabia. Whichever point of view one wishes to take, it must be remembered that Muhammad struggled to unite his countrymen into a coherent politico-religious group; and he succeeded. At the time of his death, virtually all of Arabia was under his control.

Arabia: The Religious World of Muhammad

Arabia is in the southern part of the Middle East. It is the largest peninsula in the world, covering almost one and a half million square miles (about one-third the size of the United States). It is bounded on the west by the Red Sea, on the east by the Persian Gulf, on the south by the Arabian Sea, and on the north by the Syrian desert. Because it is bounded by seas on three sides and by the Euphrates River on the north, the Arabs call it the "Island of the Arabs."

In ancient times there was no single name to denote the area, nor any single name for its population. People were referred to by group or tribe names associated with various areas. Paleolithic sites exist in both north and south Arabia, but the remains reveal little about those earliest inhabitants. Precisely when Arab people appear in history is also uncertain. [2] Numerous allusions in the Old Testament refer to peoples and places in Arabia (e.g., Isaiah 21:13; Jeremiah 25:24; Ezekiel 27:21; 2 Chronicles 9:14). Most of them, however, seem to suggest a definite distinction between north and south Arab tribes.

Nomadic life was dominant in the north, while organized settled life developed in the south. The social unit of the nomad ("bedouin," from Arabic plural *badawin*) is the tribe, named after an eponymous ancestor. Love of freedom, herding, seasonal migration, and raiding has always been the lifestyle of the nomad. The traditional beast of burden is the camel. By contrast, settled people in the south developed among other things trade, commerce, art, architecture and literature. A sense of difference, even antipathy, between north and south Arab tribes seems to have existed from the earliest times. This antipathy between northern and southern tribes caused by their differing traditions continued for a while under Islam.

Arab nomads indiscriminately preyed on everyone and each other. Trading and raiding formed the basis of their social and economic life, and their highest loyalty was to the tribe or clan, each group claiming descent from a common ancestor. Their literary heritage consisted of declamatory poems celebrating the heroic deeds of the tribe preserved through an oral tradition of recitation. Offering sacrifices and going on pilgrimages constituted their chief religious activities, and certain sites and towns considered to be holy became centers of pilgrimage and of religious ceremonies. This was especially true of Mecca, to which various tribes flocked annually.

Before the rise and expansion of Islam in the seventh century, Arabia was the scene of political instability and economic chaos. By the sixth century, the thousand-year-old civilization of Yemen had collapsed. The Ethiopians (Abyssinians), Christianized by missionaries from Roman Egypt in the fourth century, launched an invasion to dominate south Arabia in the hope of controlling the lucrative caravan trade that supplied the spices of India and the incense of Arabia to the Mediterranean world. South Arabians had appealed to their neighbours, the Persian Sassanid Empire, for help. Arabia's other neighbour, the Byzantine Empire, backed the Ethiopians. Incessant warfare between these two powerful neighbours exhausted the military strength of even the most powerful Arab chieftains. They were so drained of resources that conflict was limited to fighting among themselves.

Among the sedentary inhabitants of the peninsula, the tribe of Quraysh was relatively prosperous and enjoyed a favoured position. They inhabited Mecca and controlled the caravan trade, in spite of the threat from Ethiopia, and they skillfully, promoted the status of a sacred, cube-shaped shrine known as the Ka'bah. In the shrine was a black stone traditionally believed to have been brought down to the biblical Abraham by the angel Gabriel, a stone so holy according to legend that its pure white radiance drew pilgrims to Mecca like a beacon until human wickedness turned it black.

Because of this shrine, Mecca, long before the days of the prophet Muhammad, had been a sacred center to which Arabs came annually on a pilgrimage. Because Mecca came to be regarded as sacrosanct territory, other Arab tribes hesitated to attack it. Instead, they came to worship and to trade, to the obvious advantage of the custodians of the holy place. In spite of its favored position, rival factions did threaten Mecca from time to time, shattering its peace with intertribal quarrels and senseless bloodshed, in the avowed interests of religion.

A few steps away from the Ka'bah is the Zamzam well, believed to contain healing properties and reputed to be connected with the biblical Hagar and Ishmael. The Islamic story is that when Abraham abandoned Hagar, she wandered with her son Ishmael in the barren desert in search of water. In desperation, she left her exhausted son Ishmael lying on the hot ground while she ran back and forth in search of water. In the meantime, Ishmael tossed restlessly until his heels accidentally uncovered the opening to the well. Hagar and her son decided to settle there, and, in time, the children and grandchildren of Ishmael multiplied to become the Arab race. It is for this reason that Arabs consider themselves "sons" of Abraham through Ishmael.

Today, a building surrounds the Zamzam well. Adjacent to it is a marble tank filled with well-water so that pilgrims can drink. The water is so greatly valued that some pilgrims soak their shrouds in it or carry it home in bottles.

In addition to Arab tribes, there were Jewish and Christian settlements in Arabia. Their superior knowledge of agriculture and irrigation and their energy and industry made them prosperous enough to arouse the envy of many of their Arab neighbours. In fact, their competitive presence in the social and economic life of Arabia often threatened the trade and finance of the Meccan Arabs as well as of other townsmen.

Although the influence of Judaism and Christianity extended throughout Arabia, the religion of the Arabs was by and large animistic and polytheistic. They worshipped whatever they found awesome or mystical, such as stones, rocks, trees, and stars, and they hung rags, scraps of clothing, and other personal belongings on the branches of sacred trees, either to ward off evil or to receive some sort of divine blessing. Similar cults were associated with sources of water. Drinking, gambling and dancing were common features of most of their religious ceremonies.

There were probably many more minor gods and goddesses whose names and significance were soon forgotten under the impact of Islam, and the lack of evidence is probably no accident. Muhammad and his followers effectively put an end to all idol worship and its associated practices. No other Arab had ever succeeded in uniting his countrymen as Muhammad had. Who, then, was Muhammad and what role did he play among his countrymen? Did he believe that he was chosen to deliver the final message of God, or did his followers assume so? Perhaps it will be useful to present the life of Muhammad based on the traditional Muslim accounts.

Traditional Account

According to tradition Muhammad ibn 'Abdullah was born in Mecca around 570 CE.[3] His father 'Abdullah ('Abd Allah) belonged to the Quraysh tribe of the Hashim clan and died a few days before Muhammad's birth. Muhammad's mother Aminah died when he was only six years old. Two years later his grandfather 'Abd al-Muttalib, who was taking care of him, died too. At the age of eight, he was entrusted to his paternal uncle, Abu Talib, who was the head of the clan.

If one discounts the anecdotal details characteristic of many pious traditions, then little is known with certainty of the early life and circumstances of Muhammad. He is reputed to have accompanied his uncle Abu Talib on trading journeys to Syria. At the age of twenty-five, he was in charge of caravan transhipment of the merchandise of a wealthy widow named Khadijah, of the Asad clan. So impressed was Khadijah by Muhammad's moral qualities that she offered herself to him in marriage, even though she was fifteen years older than he was. Muhammad accepted the offer. They had two sons who died young and four daughters of whom the best known is Fatimah. Until Khadijah's death in 619, Muhammad took no other wife. His marriage gave him financial independence, since by Arab custom Muhammad as a minor had no share in the property of his father or grandfather.

Khadijah's wealth gave Muhammad the freedom to pursue his spiritual inclinations, which prompted him periodically to wander into the hills, especially into a cave outside Mecca, for meditation and contemplation. Tradition states that on one such visit around the year 610 (when he was forty years old), Muhammad had a vision of a majestic being (later identified as the angel Gabriel) and heard a voice saying to him, "Muhammad, you are God's messenger." Terrified and overwhelmed by this divine apparition, Muhammad fell prostrate. The voice commanded, "Recite!" Then Muhammad asked in terror: "What shall I recite?" And the answer came:

> Recite – in the name of your Lord who created,
> created man from clots of blood!
> Recite – for your Lord is most beneficent,
> who has taught the use of the pen,
> has taught man that which he knew not.
>
> (Sura 96:1–4)

Muhammad is said to have rushed home and told his wife Khadijah that he was either possessed (mad) or had received a prophetic call. On hearing the full story, his wife, convinced of his prophetic call, reassured him. This marked the beginning of Muhammad's career as God's messenger (Arabic, *rasul'ullah*). From this time until his death in 632 he received at frequent intervals verbal messages (or revelations) which he believed came directly from God.

It is said that as time went on Muhammad felt physical discomfort, such as perspiring on a cold day, whenever he experienced one of these divine revelations. Muhammad, like the biblical prophets, apparently suffered the physical constraints that accompany divine messages. All his doubts must have vanished when fresh messages came to him, culminating in the command to proclaim publicly what he had been taught by God.

> God
> There is no god but He, the living, the everlasting!
> Slumber seizes Him not, neither sleep.
> To Him belongs all that is in the heavens and the earth.
>
> (Sura 2:255)

Those messages were sometimes written down and sometimes memorized by his followers. Ultimately, they were collected and put into writing around 650 CE. in the form that has endured to this day and is recognized as the Qur'an.

Like the biblical prophets, Muhammad regarded himself a warner or admonisher and proclaimed his revelations to his countrymen. He emphasized four issues:

- oneness of God
- goodness and power of God
- moral responsibility of humans toward God
- judgment awaiting humanity on the day of resurrection

From the beginning, his public messages won a sympathetic audience. As he continued to preach against idolatry and advocate the worship of one God only, the number of his followers increased. Soon, his movement was called "Islam" (submission, peace) and its adherents "Muslims", though the Qur'an speaks of them simply as "the believers".

Muhammad's messages were basically religious, but his teaching implied his disapproval of the conduct and attitudes of wealthy countrymen. As a result, the rich merchants of Mecca approached Muhammad to make a deal with him. They offered him a marriage alliance with one of the wealthiest families and a substantial share in the trade if he modified his criticism. Muhammad decisively rejected both offers, which invited the hostility of the Meccans.

The opposition against Muhammad took on different forms. A person by the name of 'Amr ibn Hisham, commonly known as Abu Jahl (literally meaning "father of ignorance") organized a boycott against the members of Muhammad's clan that lasted for three years. Commercial sanctions were imposed on Muhammad's supporters, and some of his adherents were persecuted. He himself was publicly abused and ridiculed for his assertions about resurrection and the day of judgment. In fact, Muhammad would have been killed but for the protection afforded by his uncle Abu Talib, head of the clan, who nevertheless begged him to abandon his teaching.

The nature and extent of the persecution of early Muslims is difficult to assess. Clan loyalties, economic interests, political stability, and other issues affected the strength and the source of various kinds of opposition. A turning point came with the death of Abu Talib and Khadijah in 619, which meant the end of Muhammad's protection. Abu Lahab, another uncle of Muhammad, succeeded as head of the clan, and at the instigation of wealthy Meccans he withdrew the protection previously accorded Muhammad. This meant that Muhammad could no longer propagate his religion publicly without the risk of being attacked. He therefore sought the protection of inhabitants in neighboring towns where his fame had spread.

In 621, a delegation of twelve men came from Medina (Yathrib) to Mecca for the annual pilgrimage of the Ka'bah. But these men secretly professed themselves Muslims and returned to Medina in the hope of promoting the religion of Muhammad. The following year, a representative group of seventy-five persons came from Medina to Mecca, again for the annual pilgrimage of the Ka'bah. This second group invited Muhammad to Medina and pledged to defend him as they would their own kin. Encouraged by this unexpected turn of events, Muhammad accepted the offer and sent his faithful followers in small groups to Medina. Then, just before he was to leave, the Meccans, it is said, plotted to kill him. But he escaped by using little-known paths, and he reached safety in Medina on September 24, 622.

This emigration (Arabic *hijrah*; Latin *hegira*) is regarded among Muslims as the turning point not only in the development of Islam, but in world history as well. Indeed, the success of Muhammad's religion is in no little measure due to his decision to migrate to Medina. Muhammad quickly won the Arab inhabitants of Medina over to his faith.

The economic interests of Muhammad and his followers depended at first on local trade. Later, however, Muhammad approved raids, in normal Arab fashion, on caravans passing through or near Medina. He himself led three such raids in 623, all of which failed. A year later, he led some three hundred men in an attack on a wealthy Meccan caravan returning from Syria with a supporting force of more than nine hundred men. The two forces faced each other near a place called Badr, and in the ensuing battle the Meccans were badly defeated. This success appeared to Muhammad as a divine vindication of his prophetic call. Moreover, it encouraged him to lead larger Muslim forces on pre-emptive raids against hostile nomadic tribes.

Meanwhile, the Meccans determined to avenge their defeat. On March 23, 625, some three thousand Meccan infantry under the leadership of Abu Sufyan arrived at Uhud, a hill outside Medina, and faced Muhammad in a battle that ended inconclusively with heavy losses on both sides. Muhammad was wounded, but the rumour spread that he had been killed. This military reverse was a blow to Muhammad's credibility, and it forced him to regain gradually the confidence of his followers. He was also committed to a war of attrition with the men of Mecca. There was no turning back.

Muhammad took the initiative once more. He forced the Medinese Jewish tribe of Qaynuqa to emigrate to Syria, because they had refused to acknowledge his prophetic call and probably had conspired with the Meccans. In fact, in 627, Abu Sufyan, at the instigation of the Khaybar Jews and with the help of nomadic tribes, raised an army of ten thousand men in the hope of occupying Medina. Muhammad ordered the digging of ditches (or trenches) to defend exposed approaches to the city before the Meccan cavalry arrived to lay siege. Unsuccessful attempts to cross the ditches, dissension among the besiegers, and one final disastrous night of wind and rain forced the Meccan army to withdraw after only a two-week siege. In the aftermath of the withdrawal Muhammad attacked the Medinese Jewish clan of Qurayzah because they had plotted against him. All males were executed and women and children were sold as slaves.

Next, Muhammad devised a strategic plan to take Mecca without bloodshed and to convert its inhabitants to Islam. Based on a carefully calculated risk (or as tradition states, in response to a dream), Muhammad ordered his followers to march to Mecca to perform the annual rite of pilgrimage. But he was disappointed that only one thousand six hundred men would accompany him. Nevertheless, he proceeded to execute his plan with his faithful group. The date was March 628, a date celebrated in Islamic history as the "Treaty of al-Hudaybiya."

Muhammad and his followers halted at al-Hudaybiya, near Mecca, since some Meccans were determined to prevent, by force if necessary, the entrance into Mecca of this formidable and suspect force of pilgrims. Fortunately, this critical standoff did not last long. The Meccans sent a delegation to negotiate a treaty with Muhammad. According to the pact, hostilities were to end and Muslims were to postpone the performance of the pilgrimage rite to the following year. Muhammad's farsightedness as a statesman is evident in his immediate acceptance of these conditions, even though some of his followers did not agree.

To compensate disaffected followers for the withdrawal from the gates of Mecca, Muhammad led them two months later against the Khaybar Jews, then settled in the territory north of Medina. When the Khaybar Jews surrendered, Muhammad allowed them to remain in their settlement on the condition that they pay a tribute of half their total produce. He followed this profitable precedent at one neighboring Jewish settlement after another without meeting much resistance. Muhammad's policies resulted in more converts and in substantial material gain, and his fame spread far and wide as his political power grew.

Meanwhile, a number of factors helped Muhammad succeed in his ultimate aim: the taking of Mecca. Abu Sufyan was replaced by several new, weak leaders who accomplished little for the Meccans. The treaty of al-Hudaybiya lifted the threat to Meccan caravans of further retaliatory raids from Muhammad's Medinese and swung the pendulum of opinion in favor of Muhammad. Several leading families emigrated to Medina and became Muslims, and Muhammad married a widowed daughter of Abu Sufyan, thus strengthening his ties with the Meccans. This new relationship led Muhammad to plan with his father-in-law, Abu Sufyan, for the peaceful surrender of Mecca.

In March of the following year, Muhammad, accompanied by a large force of devoted followers, entered Mecca according to the provisions of the treaty. He circumambulated the Ka'bah seven times and touched the cubical black stone with his staff. Then followed the offering of sacrifices and the call to prayer. In accordance with the treaty, he was allowed to remain three days, during which time he married the sister-in-law of his uncle, al-'Abbas, after being reconciled with him.

This truce did not last long however. In November 629 the Meccans attacked one of the Arab tribes who had made an alliance with the Muslims. After two months of secret preparations, Muhammad, at the head of some ten thousand men, encamped outside Mecca. The Meccans, represented by Abu Sufyan and other leaders, negotiated for a peaceful surrender. A general amnesty was promised by Muhammad if the Meccans would formally submit. Virtually no resistance was offered and Muhammad entered Mecca in triumph, both as a statesman and as the prophet of God.

Muhammad spent about three weeks in Mecca settling various matters of administration. All idols in the Ka'bah and in neighbouring shrines were destroyed. He then entrusted the sacred territories to their traditional hereditary custodians and confirmed others in their old offices. To the poorest among his followers, he invited wealthy Meccans to grant loans. Many adopted his religion, even though he himself did not insist on their becoming Muslims.

Soon, a large force of Meccans fought side by side with his faithful Medinese companions in the face of new threats and opportunities. Indeed, Muhammad shared the spoils of every fresh success so generously with the Meccans that his Medinese complained of unfair treatment.

Militarily, Muhammad was the strongest man in Arabia. Many nomadic chiefs pledged their allegiance to him and offered their men for his raids. Several tribes sent representatives to negotiate alliances. Poets who had once ridiculed him praised his actions in laudatory verses. His armies reached northwards to Byzantine areas occupied by Christianized Arabs. Though it is difficult to know how much territory was unified under the banner of Islam, the evidence suggests that Muhammad moved quickly and effectively against armed opposition in Arabia on the one or two occasions when it was offered.

Muhammad devoted the last years of his life to consolidating the nascent Islamic community. Various observances, such as fasting, pilgrimage, the veiling of women, and providing alms tax, were all institutionalized and given the sanction of Qur'anic revelation. Moreover, he firmly prohibited his followers from fighting each other. He developed a confessional pride and communal solidarity that has hardly been surpassed by other religious founders. He insisted that the Islamic community accept the social and moral obligation of permitting "the people of the book" (those who believed in God, revelation, and scripture, such as Jews and Christians) to live freely among them and under their protection provided they accepted the Islamic social system and paid their taxes. Muhammad thus secured their allegiance and their skills as farmers, merchants, and artisans.

Although at first Muhammad was simply the head of one of the component groups existing in Medina, ten years later, by the time of his death in 632, an astonishingly large number of Arabs who professed Islam acknowledged him as leader. In fact, from a mere city-state in Medina, the Islamic community had become a "super-tribe", a confederation of Arab tribes bound by their Islamic faith rather than by blood kinship.

Muhammad went on pilgrimage to Mecca for the last time in March 632. When he returned to Medina he made preparations for an expedition to the Syrian border. Before he could leave, his health gave way and he lay sick for several days. On June 8, 632, he died, leaving the entire Muslim community in mourning.

Unlike most religions, which grew slowly from remote beginnings, Islam took shape within the lifetime of Muhammad and spread with the speed and force of a hurricane. For a quarter of a century after Muhammad's death (632 CE), the leadership continued successively by four Caliphs (from Arabic word meaning "Successors"): Abu Bakr, Omar, Uthman and 'Ali. Under their skilled leadership Islam in less than thirty years (635–651 CE) overran, Egypt, Palestine, Syria, Iraq and the Persian Empire. This successful momentum of conquest carried Islam eastwards to India as far as the borders of China, and westwards to the Atlantic, across the Straits of Gibraltar into Spain, Portugal, and France. At last, in 733 CE, one hundred years after Muhammad's death, the Muslims were halted at Tours by the Franks.

It is not certain whether Muhammad could read or write, but almost from the start his followers took down what he recited, using scraps of parchment and leather, tablets of stone, ribs of palm branches, and anything else they could find to write on. Soon after Muhammad's death, those fragments were collected and called the Qur'an.

Principal Sources

Our principal source of information on Muhammad is the Qur'an, the sacred book of the Islamic religion.[4] The Qur'an (Arabic word meaning "recitation" formed in *ca.* 650 CE) is regarded as the final message of God transmitted to Muhammad through the angel Gabriel from an original preserved in heaven. Thus, all of its 114 chapters (called *suras* in Arabic) are believed to be eternal and uncreated.

While the followers of Islam respect the scriptures of Judaism and Christianity, they regard the Qur'an as the pure and final essence of divine revelation, superseding the other scriptures. Its inspiration and authority are thought to extend to every letter and title (of which there are 323,621) so that every Muslim must read the Qur'an in Arabic. Although the Qur'an has been translated into some forty languages, it is believed to lose much of its inspiration in translation; no translation has ever fully conveyed the eloquence or flavour of the original Arabic.

Five important teachings stand out clearly in the Qur'an (see Sura 2:176): To believe in God, the Last Day, the Angels, the Book, and the Prophets. The importance of the concept of the Prophets is as great as the principle that proclaims the Oneness of God. Thus, the Muslim ideal is based on the life of Muhammad and the Qur'an.

The Qur'an has a fixed content that was codified about twenty-five years after the death of Muhammad. Yet it tells very little about the "life" of Muhammad. His name is mentioned four or five times (once as Ahmad). Two other important points that can be inferred from the Qur'an are that Muhammad spent most of his life in western Arabia, and that he bitterly resented those who opposed his claim of a prophet. However, additional information about Muhammad's "life" derives from two different types of sources: Muslim and non-Muslim. The Muslim sources are written in Arabic and include (1) casual allusions in the Qur'an and (2) oral traditions collected and written down by Muslim scholars (called Hadith). The non-Muslim sources are preserved in the literatures of Jewish and Christian communities written in Greek, Syriac, Armenian, and Hebrew.

The traditional accounts of Muhammad's life derive from Muslim scholars who collected and wrote down his biographies one or two centuries after his death. The accuracy of these biographies, though unascertainable, is accepted by many, though not all, scholars. Muhammad died in 632 and the earliest material on his life derives from Ibn Ishaq (d. 768). The question of authenticity is problematic because the original work of Ibn Ishaq is lost. What is available is only an edited version of Ibn Ishaq by Ibn Hisham (d. 834). Other Muslim sources of information include Ma'mar ibn Rashid (d. 770), Sayf ibn 'Umar (d. *ca.* 796), al-Waqidi (d. 823), al-Baladhuri (d. 829), Muhammad ibn Sa'd (d. 843), and al-Tabari (d. 923).

In addition to the sources transmitted within the Muslim tradition, there are a few non-Muslim sources, all of whom confirm the existence of Muhammad. None of these materials are considered to be from before 634 C.E., and much that is of interest is from some decades later. An Armenian chronicler attests that Muhammad was a merchant and that his teaching revolved around the figure of Abraham. The Greek and Syriac materials confirm that the followers of the "new" religion are known as *magaritai* (in Greek) or *mahgraye* (in Syriac). Those terms refer to the Arabic term *muhajirun* (the "emigrants"), denoting Muhammad and his followers who migrated from Mecca to Yathrib (later known as Medina) in 622 CE.

It must be stated, however, that the information preserved in both the Muslim traditions and the non-Muslim sources contain some essential differences. A few are chronological (e.g., the founding of Muhammad's community); others relate to Muhammad's attitude toward the Jews and Palestine.

Naturally, those diverse sources of information are not all of equal importance, even though each has a certain intrinsic value. The Qur'an stands foremost in importance. The Muslim traditions, as a rule, rank next to the Qur'an, while the remaining sources provide especially valuable corroboration of the statements in the Qur'an and the Muslim traditions.

Although this ranking may at first seem convincing, it is not free from difficulties. The difficulties become evident when an attempt is made to resolve the life and teachings of Muhammad. Does the Qur'an retain the essential features of the original teachings of Muhammad, or does it derive its authority from "faithfully pre-served" later traditions? And how is one to explain the disagreements between the Muslim tradition and the non-Muslim sources?

These questions have long been the subject of dispute among scholars. Critical investigation of the material on Muhammad, both in the Qur'an and in the mass of Muslim traditions, has resulted in profound scholarly disagreements concerning his life or the part he played in early Muslim community. In fact, the attempt to separate the historical from the unhistorical elements in the available sources has yielded few, if any, positive results regarding the figure of Muhammad or the role he played in Islam.

From among the diverse opinions, two extreme views are worth noting: those that cast doubt on the historicity of Muhammad and the integrity of the Qur'an; and those that portray Muhammad based on the Qur'an and traditional Muslim biographies.

An Assessment

A balanced understanding and interpretation of the nature, role, and contribution of Muhammad is not an easy task. Muhammad's focus of interest during all these years had been the training, education, and discipline of the Muslim community. His moral, social, and political influence remained long after he left the scene. It is not always easy to distinguish with confidence genuine tradition from later accretions. Though Muhammad has suffered greatly both from critics and from apologetic writers, nobody who studies the life of Muhammad can fail to be impressed by two of his most dominant characteristics: spiritual leadership and political acumen.

The view that he was a political genius (or a great statesman) as well as a spiritual guide (or a religious leader) is testified in the Qur'an, in the Islamic Traditions, and in historical sources.[5] Certainly, Muhammad participated in social life in its fullest. He married, had a household, judged, ruled, raided, fought many battles and underwent painful ordeals. He was human enough to become engrossed in the solutions to social, economic, and political problems. But Muhammad was also a pious, contemplative person. He spent long periods in solitude and meditation, seeking peace and divine revelation, and he believed that he was commissioned specifically to propagate God's message to humanity.

Muhammad prescribed certain specific directives regarding religious rights and practices, but it provided neither a systematic exposition of beliefs nor a consistent body of doctrine. At best, it presented a number of brief and variant statements on faith, piety, and practice. Two important passages in the Qur'an illustrate what constitutes Islamic piety, belief and disbelief:

> True piety is this: to believe in God, and the Last Day, the Angels, the Book, and the Prophets. (Qur'an 2.176)

> O believers believe in God, and in His Messenger, and in the Book which he has sent down to his Messenger, and the Book which he sent down previously. For whosoever disbelieves in God, and his Angels, and His Books, and His Messengers, and the Last Day, has indeed strayed far in error. (Qur'an 4.135–136)

Five important teachings are immediately apparent in those scriptural declarations: God, Angels, Books, Prophets, and the Last Day – commonly called "Articles of Faith."

God Of the five tenets central to Islam, the foremost is the oneness of God. "There is no other god but God" is an assertion that Muhammad stressed, and he rejected the Christian concept of the Trinity as being polytheistic (Qur'an 4.168–69; 5.78; 112.1). He was unequivocal on that point. For Muhammad (and all Muslims) there is only one God, who exists from eternity to all eternity. He is all-seeing, all-hearing, all-speaking, all-knowing, all-willing, all-powerful, and above all, an absolute unity. Thus, everything comes into being through God's divine will and creative word. He is the creator, provider, and protector of humanity and the universe. Consider the following selections:

> God, there is no god but He, the living, the everlasting! Slumber seizes Him not, neither sleep; to Him belongs all that are in the heavens and the earth. Who is there that shall intercede with Him except by his permission? He knows what lies before them and what is after them; and they comprehend not anything of His knowledge except such as He wills. His throne comprises the heavens and the earth; the preserving of them oppresses Him not; He is the all-high, the all-glorious. (Qur'an 2.255–256)

> All that is in the heavens and the earth magnifies God. He is the all-mighty, the all-wise. To Him belongs the kingdom of the heavens and the earth. He gives life, and He makes to die, and He is powerful over everything. He is the first and the last, the outward and the inward. He has knowledge of everything. It is He that created the heavens and the earth in six days, then seated Himself upon the Throne. He knows what penetrates into the earth and what comes forth from it, what comes down from heaven, and what goes up into it. He is with you wherever you are; and God sees the things you do. To Him belongs the kingdom of the heavens and the earth; and unto Him all matters are returned. He makes the night to enter into the day and makes the day to enter into the night. He knows the thoughts within the breasts. (Qur'an 57.1–5)

Angels A second fundamental tenet is belief in intermediary beings called angels, two of whom play especially prominent roles: Gabriel, who appeared before Muhammad to reveal to him that he had been called by God, and *Iblis*, or *Shaitan* (Satan), who along with the *jinn* (rebellious angels) are destined to be judged and condemned to hell. Angels,.like humans, are created by God; but unlike humans, they are sexless, immortal, and resplendent, created of light to inhabit the invisible world. They are God's messengers, exercising a potent influence on both the life of humans and the life of the universe.

> Praise be to God, Creator of the heavens and the earth, who

appointed the angels as messengers, having wings, two, three, and four . . . (Qur'an 35.1)

Everything in the heavens and every creature crawling on earth and the angels, bow to God. (Qur'an 14.51)

In addition, angels are said to act as intermediaries asking God to forgive the offenses of believers (Qur'an 40.7). At the time of death, the souls of humans are received by angels (Qur'an 6.93; 8.52; 16.30; 47.29) who have kept a record of their actions (Qur'an 6.61; 43.80; 82.10) and will witness for or against them on the Day of Judgement (Qur'an 21.103; 13.24; 33.43). One angel who arrogantly refused to honour Adam resulted in his fall from divine grace. He was anathematized as Satan, and his role was reduced to leading humans astray to commit errors and offenses (Qur'an 15.28–43). Associated with angels, but quite distinct from them, are the genies, *jinn* (singular, *jinni*), created of fire.

We [God] created man from clay of moulded mud; but We created the *jinn* earlier from the *samum* [i.e. fire of the scorching wind]. (Qur'an 15.26–7)

I [God] have not created *jinn* and mankind except to serve me. I do not desire any provision from them, nor do I desire that they should feed me. (Qur'an 51.56–7)

Books The third principal teaching is the sacredness of the Qur'an. Muslims believe there is a celestial archetype of scripture, often called the Preserved Tablet, or the Mother of the Book (Qur'an 13.39; 85.21), from which God revealed his message, as necessity arose, through the angel Gabriel to various prophets in succession. Whenever chaos, confusion, or evil suffused human society, God sent a fresh message to urge people to repent and renew their submission to him. God's messages, then, are really one, and the role of each successive messenger is simply to confirm the messages that have gone before. Three Books preceded the Qur'an: the Torah, Psalms, and Gospels. Although they are to be regarded as Holy Scriptures, Muslims consider the Qur'an God's final revelation, superseding all previous revelations. Its message is addressed to all humanity, including Jews and Christians, who are thought to belong to a community defined as the "People of the Book."

Prophets The fourth important teaching is belief in the prophets. The importance of the prophets is as crucial as the oneness of God. Islam maintains that God has communicated his divine message and guidance to humanity throughout the ages through the medium of selected members of the human race — the prophets (or messengers) of God. (According to Islamic theology, a messenger (*rasul*) is thought to rank a grade higher than a prophet (*nabi*). A messenger is one who is sent by God to a special community with a Book (Scripture) containing rules and laws for human conduct. A prophet merely preaches a message. Prophets are not messengers, but all messengers also are prophets.)

Muslims honour a total of twenty-eight messengers of God beginning with Adam and continuing with, among others, Abraham, Noah, Moses, and Jesus. All of those men were selected by God to convey the divine messages to keep humanity on the right track. At a particular point in history Muhammad was selected as the last messenger and commanded to convey God's complete design to the entire human race. Thus, Muhammad is thought of as the seal of the prophets, through whom God revealed his eternal message in its definitive form.

The Last Day The fifth teaching that occupies an important place is the Day of Judgment. Heaven, hell, and the final Day of Judgment are described elaborately and powerfully. Every individual will be called to account. A resurrection of the body, a final judgment, and a final destiny in heaven or hell, depending on one's record on earth, will occur.

The vivid descriptions of heaven and hell and the elaborate portrayal of the final judgment are very similar to the Book of Revelation in the New Testament, and yet more powerful. The events of the last day are described as cataclysmic, that is, as appearing suddenly with great cosmic changes and at a time known only to God. On that day, when the trumpet sounds, the sun shall be darkened, the stars shall fall, the heavens shall be split asunder, the mountains shall turn to dust, and the earth shall be crushed.

When the sun shall be darkened,
When the stars shall be thrown down,
When the mountains shall be set moving,
When the pregnant camels shall be neglected,
When the savage beasts shall be mustered,

When the seas shall be set boiling . . .
When the heavens shall be stripped off,
When hell shall be set blazing,
When paradise shall be brought nigh,
Then shall a soul know what it has produced!
(Qur'an 81.1–14)

On that last day the graves will open, and humanity will be called to account. The guardian angel of each individual will bear witness to that person's record on earth. Each person's deeds will be weighed in the divine balance, and a "book" containing one's record of life will be placed in one's hand. If the book is placed in the right hand, the individual will be among the blessed; if the book is placed in the left hand, the individual will be among the damned.

Then as for him who is given his book in his right hand . . . he shall be in a pleasing life, in a lofty garden . . . . But as for him who is given his book in his left hand, he shall say, "Would that I had not been given my book and not known my reckoning! Would it had been the end! Take him and fetter him, and then roast him in Hell! (Qur'an 69.13–37)

In conclusion, one must recognize that Muhammad sought constantly to perform the will of God, and in fact his participation in social and political activities was precisely to integrate those areas into a spiritual whole. In addition, assessors of Muhammad by and large agree on his tremendous achievements in developing the dual religious and social character of Islam. It is said, for instance, that as the founder of a state, and of a religion, Muhammad made the religion of Islam the basis of Arab confederation and unity. Again, one reads that from the very beginning, Muhammad inculcated among his followers a sense of brotherhood and a bond of faith unmatched in any other religious or social group.[6] Be that as it may, the Qur'an repeatedly disclaims all superhuman characteristics for Muhammad. He is like all human beings, a mortal person. Yet, unlike most individuals, he is commissioned with the sole duty of conveying God's final message to all humanity. Also, his pronouncements on all matters in life are to be accepted as divine revelation and in one sense "infallible." Obedience to his message is submission to God.

4
Zoroaster

One day, at dawn, when Zoroaster was standing peacefully by the river Daiti, he was met by an archangel who asked him what was his supreme desire, to which Zoroaster replied: "Sing, praise, and devote myself to God."

On receiving Zoroaster's reply, the archangel led Zoroaster to the presence of God . . . Then Zoroaster said, "O Wise Lord . . . reveal unto me for my enlightenment that which you have ordained as the better path for me to follow, so that I may join myself unto it."

(YASNA 31.5)

Zoroastrianism is the religion of a tiny ethno-religious community that still resides in its ancient homeland in modern Iran. Some Zoroastrians migrated from Iran during the ninth and tenth centuries CE and settled on the west coast of India. Their number at present is still small, and they are popularly known as Parsees (or Parsis), a name that refers to the province of Fars in ancient Persia. Since the rise of European imperialism, Zoroastrians from both Iran and India have migrated and established small communities in almost every major city in the West.

Thus, of the great religious founders, Zarathustra (known to us through the Greeks as Zoroaster) is certainly one of the least known. This statement may come as a surprise to those who are not familiar with the incalculable influence of Zoroaster's ideas on other religions, especially Judaism, Christianity and Islam. The ideas of the devil, Satan, the adversary, and the vivid imagery of heaven and hell all stem from Zoroaster. His tendency to favour a belief in one God (monotheism) and his teaching of the continual struggle between good and evil (dualism), affected contemporary religious practices. Moreover, down through the ages, the indirect but powerful contribution of Zoroastrian ideas has been seen in a number of literary classics: Dante's *Divine Comedy*, Adamnan's *Vision of Heaven and Hell*, and Milton's *Paradise Lost*.

In a brief study such as this, however, it is impossible to give an accurate idea of the pervasive influence that Zoroaster and his ideas have had in shaping the patterns of modern world religions. Suffice it to say that the impact of Zoroaster was so forceful that the religion which he left has ever since borne his name. Let us start then by considering first the religious milieu in which Zoroaster lived.

Persia (Iran): The Religious World of Zoroaster

Northwest of India, close to the Caspian Sea, there lived many centuries ago a group of wanderers who were of the same race as the Vedic Aryans.[1] At some point during the second millennium BCE, one group of those Aryan invaders went to India (Hinduism developed in this group), and another entered present-day Armenia, Azerbaijan and the Iranian plateau   an area that historians sometimes prefer to call Persia.[2]

The religion of the Persians was similar in many respects to the Vedic religion in India. Many of the gods worshipped in Persia were similar to the gods of India. Prominent among the deities were nature gods such as Sky: Vivahvant (Vedic Vavasvant); Wind: Vayu (Vedic Vayu); Sun: Mithra (Vedic Mitra); Water: Haurvatat (Vedic Sarvatat); Fire: Atar (Vedic Agni), and so on. Along with those gods there were innumerable good and evil spirits that were invoked and worshipped. Such were Death: Yima (Vedic Yama); Truth: Asha (Vedic Rta); Immortality: Ameretat (Vedic Amrta), and the like.

The central ritual of the Persian religion consisted of at least three forms of sacrifices: the animal sacrifice, the libation (drink) sacrifice, and the fire sacrifice. The animal and libation sacrifices seemed to have been combined into one ritual, and the available evidence suggests this ritual was something of a drunken orgy. The traditional ritual consisted of slaughtering a bull or ox while the attending priests shouted and danced. During this ceremony, the priests also performed the libation rite in which they squeezed the juice from the haoma plant (in Vedic, the soma plant) and formally drank it, sometimes sharing the drink with worshippers. This juice must have been fermented and was certainly intoxicating, because Zoroaster condemned the priests for what he described as their filthy drunkenness and for their attempts to deceive the people.

The priests who performed the ceremonies and who claimed that they could control and influence the benevolent and malevolent spirits, came to be called Magi.[3] The method by which they practiced their art was called magic. They not only claimed to influence divine powers in order to control everyday events, but were experts in the occult sciences. They interpreted dreams, received and delivered omens, foretold future events, read signs through the movements of stars or the flight of birds, and practised various kinds of divination.

The problem of identifying the Magi(ans) is exceedingly difficult. To begin with, the etymology of the word (Persian magu, Greek magos) is unclear. Then, the available sources (archaeological, inscriptional, literary) provide a confusing image regarding the character or activities of the Magi. It is possible that originally they arose from the priestly caste of the Medes. Later, under the Achaemenids, they performed certain rituals and ceremonies connected with fire, sacrifices, and burials (cf. Herodotus 1.101, 107, 132, 140). Still later, possibly after the contact with the Greeks and continuing up to the Islamic period in 651 CE, they may have claimed the possession of supernatural knowledge and acted as fortune-tellers, astrologers, magicians, sorcerers, tricksters, and charlatans. The story of their visit to Mary and the infant Jesus (Matthew 2:1–2) is in itself proof of their fame and influence. Thus, though their long survival testifies to their vitality, little is known about the development of or the role played by the Magi(ans).

Sometime during these dramatic and decisive events Zoroaster appeared. His life and teachings are to be found in the Zoroastrian scriptures. However, it is not easy to identify a historical figure known as Zoroaster. Indeed, there are some scholars who doubt that such a person ever lived and argue that he was simply a mythical figure created to account for a religious reform movement which developed in Persia. Most scholars, however, through the careful study of the Zoroastrian scriptures have concluded that a man called Zoroaster did exist. So, before considering the Zoroastrian scriptures, it will be useful to present the traditional story of Zoroaster.

Traditional Account

Zoroastrian tradition maintains that Zoroaster was the prophet of ancient Iran who lived in the seventh to sixth centuries BCE.[4] His birthplace was Azerbaijan, north-west of Media. His father Pourushaspa, was from the family of Spitama, whose genealogy is traced back through forty-five generations to Gayomart (the first man, like Adam), and his mother, Dughdhova, was from the clan of Hvogva (Yasna 46.13, 51.12, 53.1). Of his mother, it is said that at the age of fifteen she conceived and gave virgin birth to Zoroaster.

The traditional account of Zoroaster's infancy and later life abound with miracles. He is said to have been born laughing, instead of weeping (Denkard 7.3.2). He is also said to have escaped as an infant numerous attempts made on his life, through the intervention of beasts (Denkard 7.3.8 ff.). First, a bull stood over him to protect him from the hoofs of cattle; then a stallion saved him in the same way from being trampled by horses; and again, a she-wolf accepted him among her cubs, instead of devouring him.

Tradition, furthermore, maintains that Zoroaster was trained to be a priest (Yasna 33.6, 13.94). At the age of twenty, however, Zoroaster left home, against the wishes of his parents (Zadspram 16.1). Ten years later, his quest for truth culminated in a vision, or revelation (Yasna 43; Denkard 7.3.51; Zadspram 21.1–27). The story of this first vision, as stated in Zoroastrian tradition is as follows (Zadspram 20–21).

Zoroaster was attending the celebration of the spring festival and, according to ancient custom, fetched water at dawn from a nearby river for a sacred ritual. As he returned to the bank from mid-water, he saw the shining figure of the archangel Vohu Mana (Good Intention), who led Zoroaster to the presence of God Ahura Mazda (Wise Lord) and the five Immortals, where he was taught the cardinal principles of the "true" or "good" religion. This vision, in which Zoroaster saw, heard, or felt conscious of Ahura Mazda, was later repeated a number of times (Yasna 31.8, 33.6–7, 43.5). As a result, Zoroaster believed that he was commissioned by Ahura Mazda to teach the "good religion" (Yasna 44.11, 28.4).

Tradition states, moreover, that Zoroaster's mission started at the age of thirty, and during the next ten years he was successful in converting only one person, his cousin Maidhyoimah (Yasna 51.19; Yasht 13.95; Bundahishn 32.2; Zadspram 23.1–2). These long, discouraging years of Zoroaster brought him into sharp conflict with the priests of his day. Bitterly disappointed by their obduracy, he cried in despair to Ahura Mazda:

To what land to flee? Where shall I go to flee? They exclude (me) from my family and from my clan. The community with which I have associated has not satisfied me, nor those who are the deceitful rulers of the land. How, then, shall I satisfy thee, Ahura Mazda? (Yasna 46.1)

Suddenly a ray of hope flashed back in him as he triumphed in his own faith:

Yes, praising, I shall always worship all of you Ahura Mazda (Yasna 50.4)

Zoroaster's passionate concern for God, his witnessing of the outrageous and shameless perversion of the religious rites, his utter despair at being deserted by kindred and fellow-workers, and his own inner doubts and questionings, deeply moved Zoroaster (Yasna 46.2, 43.11, 49.1–2, 32.13–14). Like the biblical leader Joshua (Joshua 24:15) and the prophet Micah (Micah 7:7), Zoroaster's words echoed triumphantly to haunt the imagination of human beings ever after:

I choose (only) thy teachings Lord. (Yasna 46.3)

The tradition that perhaps remains as the most popular among Zoroastrians today is of Zoroaster's success in converting King Vishtaspa and the royal court in Bactria (Yasht 9.26, 13.99–100). The story is that Zoroaster, after three days of disputations at a great assembly at the royal palace, encountered the hostility of the *kavis* and *karapans* (? priests, religious leaders). These enemies arranged for Zoroaster to be cast into prison, where he remained for a while until he won the willing ear of King Vishtaspa by curing the king's favourite horse, who was paralysed (Denkard 7.4.70 ff.). Accordingly, King Vishtaspa, the queen, and the entire royal dignitaries accepted whole-heartedly Zoroaster's teachings. This event, which, according to Zoroastrian tradition, took place when Zoroaster was forty-two years old, helped the spread of his faith.

Although the problems associated with the sources make it difficult, if not impossible, to describe the spread of Zoroaster's faith, there is some evidence that Zoroaster organized, perhaps in an informal way, a fellowship or brotherhood of his followers, and that this brotherhood had certain divisions within it (Yasna 32.1, 33.3,

46.1, 49.7). Furthermore, tradition states that Zoroaster lived in a new home, married three times (this polygamous marriage is rejected by modern Zoroastrians), and had three sons and three daughters – three daughters and a son from the first wife, two sons from the second, and none from the third (Yasna 53.3; Yasht 13; Denkard 9.45; Great Bundahishn 35.56). His three sons initiated and represented the three classes of society: the priests, the warriors, and the farmers (Great Bundahishn 35.56; Indian Bundahishn 32.5). Finally, at the age of seventy-seven, Zoroaster died a violent death, though it is not known exactly how. One story is that he was assassinated while praying in the fire-temple; another states that he was slain with other priests in the fire-temple by the Turanians, who stormed the city of Balk (Denkard 5.3.2, 7.5.1; Dadistan i Dinik 72.8; Zadspram 23.9).

This traditional account raises several important questions. How reliable are the stories recorded in the Zoroastrian scriptures? In what language(s) was (were) the original text(s) written? Do these stories contain an element of political propaganda or theological beliefs produced later by Zoroastrian followers? When and by whom was the final edition/version formed? Those questions, among others, are matters of scholarly dispute which are still unresolved.

Obviously, solving those issues will produce satisfactory answers for those seeking to understand the Zoroastrian faith. Thousands of Zoroastrian devotees, however, find comfort, guidance, and inspiration in the words recorded in their sacred scripture. Thus, both tradition and scripture have positive values, and a judicious balance of those two will undoubtedly produce more rewarding results.

Principal Sources

The principal sources of information on the life and teachings of Zoroaster may be classified under two categories: Zoroastrian and non-Zoroastrian.[5] Zoroastrian sources of information consist of the Avesta (the Zoroastrian scripture, which contains the Yasna, Visparad, Videvdat, and the Yashts) and a collection of later religious documents (such as the Bundahishn, Denkard, Zadspram, and many more). The non-Zoroastrian sources of information are found in works by classical authors, mainly Greek and Roman, and references by Armenian, Syrian, Arab, Chinese, and Icelandic writers.

Naturally, these diverse sources of information are not all of equal importance, even though each has a certain intrinsic value. The Avesta, (final formation in c.370 CE), particularly the Gathas (Hymns) of Zoroaster (Yasna 28–34, 43–51, 53), stand foremost in importance. The classical references, as a rule, rank next to the Avesta, while the information provided in the remaining sources is especially valuable to substantiate the statements presented in both the Avesta and the classical writings.

While the Avesta may retain certain essential features of the original teachings, it is believed to have derived its authority from "faithfully preserved" older traditions. How much of its contents dates from the earliest period, and how much of it was rewritten to make the past agree with the realities and beliefs of the time in which it was composed is, of course, open to question. In fact, the surviving Avesta is only a fragment of the whole, and the disparity of its parts is evidence of the vicissitudes through which it went before it became crystallized to its present form.

The Gathas are considered to contain the life and teachings of Zoroaster himself, but unfortunately their archaic language creates an enormous difficulty in eliciting meaning from the obscure texts. This is best illustrated by comparing the translations of the Gathas made by several competent scholars, whose differences are quite startling.

The information preserved in the later Zoroastrian sources are usually considered as the natural continuation of the Avesta. But here, too, the ambiguity of the scripts, and the legendary material that has accrued through the centuries, create a difficulty in reconstructing the life of Zoroaster with any degree of certainty. In fact, the incongruities in the existing records have resulted in diverse opinions among scholars on almost every aspect of Zoroaster's life.

An Assessment

Although the traditional account of Zoroaster may at first seem convincing, it is in no way free from difficulties. Every scholar who has tried to study the mass of information preserved in the Zoroastrian texts knows that the endeavor to sift the evidence to arrive at some tangible historical facts results only in the most unpleasant feeling of uncertainty, because the available sources of information provide conflicting images of the prophet. These obstacles become evident when an attempt is made to understand the meaning of his name, to resolve his place and date of birth, to determine his ancestry and family, or to outline his religious beliefs and teachings.[6]

Moreover, in spite of the painstaking research in the field of Zoroastrian (or Iranian) archaeology, ethnology, philology, religious literature, and history, there is still no consensus of opinion on Zoroaster's life. This, of course, is not surprising at all, because there is a confusing mixture of fact, legend, and myth in all the sources. The task of separating trustworthy Zoroastrian tradition from fanciful lore has been pursued by reputable scholars, but while there is a large measure of agreement among these scholars, the debate is still far from being over. Thus, since we lack precise biographical data, we must be satisfied for the moment to accept the following traditional (and tentative) conclusions.

Zoroaster was born in Persia at the end of the seventh or the beginning of the sixth century BCE, the period preceding the formation of the Persian empire under Cyrus II (559–529 BCE). He was trained to be a priest, since he refers to himself as a *zaotar*, the chief priest to officiate in the ritual of sacrifice. Whether he chose his priestly function or acquired it through heredity is difficult to assess, although the former seems more likely. His father's name was Pourushaspa and his mother's Dughdova. He was married and had several children.

Furthermore, the Gathas indicate unmistakably the personal relationship – a passionate, intense dialogue Zoroaster had with his God. His spiritual visions created in him a religious zeal to proselytize, but his initial efforts at spreading "the good religion" and winning support for his views met with hostility and ultimate failure. Eventually, however, Zoroaster found a patron, King Vishtaspa, who not only accepted Zoroaster's faith, but helped propagate it throughout his kingdom. Beyond these few facts, nothing more can be said with certainty about Zoroaster's life.

What about the teachings of Zoroaster? In what way did the nature of his message differ from ancient Persian beliefs and practices? Did his teaching represent an "apparent dualism" or an "imperfect monotheism"? Did he believe that the world was ruled by two opposing principles, one good and the other evil? Or did he insist on the supremacy of one God?

These questions have long been the subject of dispute, and once again the difficultly lies in the surviving literature, the inscriptional evidence, and the archaeological finds. Nevertheless, it is possible to sketch the main lines of thought of Zoroaster within the context of ancient Persian beliefs and practices. In fact, our knowledge is further enhanced by the affinities that exist between the Persian and Indian (Vedic, Hindu) religious concepts and social customs.

There were several important Persian divinities who were either ignored, condemned, or assumed by Zoroaster. Those Persian divinities were divided between the benevolent (*ahura*) and malevolent (*daeva*) deities (reversed in Vedic pantheon, *asura* is malevolent and *deva* is benevolent). Moreover, the animal sacrifice, combined with the rite of *haoma*, must have been an unseemly and orgiastic affair accompanied by shouts of joy, because Zoroaster condemned the filthy (literally "urine") drunkenness of the priests, and their attempts to deceive the people (Yasna 48.10; cf. Herodotus 4.75). Whether Zoroaster was opposed to the ritual as such, or only to the form of the ritual, is difficult to decide.

Turning for comparison to ancient Persian religious concepts, the first in importance was *asha*, meaning truth, or order. The principle that violated *asha* was druj, meaning falsehood, or disorder. Zoroaster, who seems to have adopted this basic duality, described himself as a true enemy of the followers of *druj*, and a powerful supporter of the followers of *asha* (Yasna 43.8). These concepts of order and disorder, or truth and falsehood, belonged to the realm of nature as well as to that of cultic rites and moral law. Zoroaster asked his God to tell him who was "in the beginning the father to *asha*," to which God replied that he "the Wise One was the father of *asha*" (Yasna 44.3, 47.2).

Thus, Zoroaster's religious innovation rests on his familiarity with ancient Persian tradition and on his skill in rejecting or reformulating the beliefs and practices of that tradition. This, of course, does not belittle his achievement; on the contrary, it was quite radical, especially when seen against a polytheistic background. Indeed, the religious corruption of his day deeply offended him, particularly the base practices of the Persian priests, who through their evil actions diverted people from the best course of action and the divine purpose in life (Yasna 32.9–12). Without doubt, such were the followers of *druj*, and Zoroaster openly condemned them as the beloved of the malevolent deities (*daeva*), and obstructers of the Good Mind, departing from the divine purpose of God and from his law (Yasna 32.4, 11). That such a pronouncement would bring him into sharp conflict with the sacrificial priests, he knew very well; yet in the face of persecution, he spoke courageously against them calling them willfully blind and deaf and accusing them of hindering the noble principles of truth and good thought through their own deceitful actions and doctrines (Yasna 51.4).

Against a pantheon of Persian deities, some benevolent, others malevolent, Zoroaster held the supremacy of Ahura Mazda (Wise God/Lord), the lord of life and wisdom, the first and last for all eternity (Yasna 31.8, 43.16). Moreover, Ahura Mazda was mighty and holy, the creator of all, giver of all good, and the giver of life (Yasna 43.4, 44.7, 48.3, 50.11). To those who looked up to Ahura Mazda with awe, to them he was a friend, brother, and father (Yasna 45.11). Because Ahura Mazda was holy, eternal, just, omniscient, the primeval being, creator of all and the origin of all goodness, Zoroaster chose him as his sole God (Yasna 29.6, 43.4, 43.5, 45.3, 46.3). Thus, Zoroaster took over the ancient Persian belief in the *ahura* (benevolent gods) and transferred that belief to a sole Ahura (God/Lord) whom he saw as the Mazda (Wisdom), and who was therefore called Ahura Mazda, meaning Wise God/Lord. The relationship of Ahura Mazda to other divine powers or entities, known as y*azad* (*yazata*), described by Zoroaster is not easy to define.

According to ancient Persian belief, Ahura Mazda was the wise lord, the all-knowing sky god, and the supreme creator. He was also intimately associated with truth, sovereignty, mysterious power, light, and sun. His nature was best expressed in the cult of fire (*atar*). The ritual attached to the sacred fire existed before Zoroaster, who adopted it and made it the outward symbol of truth (Yasna 43.4, 9). In fact, Zoroaster taught that, for an individual to exercise free choice intelligently, Ahura Mazda gave his pure mind and his flaming fire of thought (Yasna 46.7). This fire was an enduring, blazing flame bringing clear guidance and joy to the true believer but destruction to lovers of evil (Yasna 34.4). It was through the energy of fire that Ahura Mazda assigned judgment to truth-followers and to evil-followers (Yasna 43.4, 47.6).

Zoroaster saw humanity as divided into two opposing parties: the truth-followers (*ashavant*), who were just and god-fearing; and the evil-followers (*dregvant*), among whom were classed all evil-rulers, evil-doers, evil-speakers, those of evil conscience, and evil-thinkers (Yasna 49.11). But this basic dualism that Zoroaster saw here and now on earth he projected to the whole cosmos. He came to see that this fundamental tension existed both in the material as well as in the spiritual spheres. Over against a transcendental good mind stood the evil mind; over against the good spirit stood the evil spirit; and so on. Yet, on every level, a choice had to be made. This insistence on freedom of choice was the marked characteristic of Zoroaster's teaching. In fact, what stood in Zoroaster's principles was not the ethical dualism of good versus evil but the importance of the individual as an arbiter between them. Each individual was ultimately faced with making a choice between good and evil, truth and falsehood.

Zoroaster's concept of dualism and free choice seems to have derived from an ancient Persian myth of two uncreated *manyu* (spirit/being): the one, the bringer of life and abundance, was good in thought, speech, and deed; the other, the author of death and destruction, was evil in thought, speech, and deed. And human beings, Zoroaster said, could exercise their freedom to follow one of the two. This is expressed with characteristic force in the following words:

> Listen with your ears to the best things. Reflect with a clear mind man by man for himself upon the two choices of decision, being aware to declare yourselves to Him before the great retribution [i.e., final judgment]. Yes, there are two fundamental spirits, twins which are renowned to be in conflict. In thought and in word, in action, they are two: the good and the bad. And between these two, the beneficent have chosen correctly, not so the maleficent. Furthermore, when these two spirits first came together, they created life and death, and how, at the end, the worst existence [i.e., hell] shall be for the deceitful, but the best thinking [i.e., heaven] for the truthful person. (Yasna 30.2–4)

Thus, side by side with the fundamental principle of freedom of choice, Zoroaster taught that the good was its own reward; that happiness and misery were the consequences of an individual's good and evil deeds (Yasna 33.2–3). He saw the final consummation of creation, at which time Ahura Mazda was to come with his three powers; that ultimately the wicked would deliver the evil/falsehood into the hands of truth; and that eternal joy would reign everywhere. Moreover, the souls of humans were to be judged at the "bridge of the judge." The just would receive their eternal reward, while the wicked, their final doom. Hell was the abode of all evil rulers, evil-doers, evil-speakers, those of evil conscience, and evil-thinkers (Yasna 46.7, 11, 9.11, 51.14). Heaven was the abode of the righteous, who would be blessed with Ahura Mazda's reward of perfection and immortality (Yasna 31.21, 32.13, 32.15, 51.15). Humans assisted the cause of Ahura Mazda by choosing good deeds, good words, and good thoughts.

Deeply rooted in Zoroaster's teaching, then, was the moral responsibility of choice. This meant that each individual held the key to his or her own destiny by exercising his or her own choice between good and evil, truth and falsehood. But the cause of truth demanded the crushing of evil. Thus, the decision to follow truth necessarily implied a commitment to Ahura Mazda, the very essence of truth, both in the moral and physical order. And it is precisely here that Zoroaster called everyone to join in combat against the forces of evil in order to bring about the ultimate triumph of Ahura Mazda and of all the eternal forces of life.

This brings us to an important and controversial question: Was Zoroaster a dualist or a monotheist? Four critical opinions have been proposed. First, some insist, that Zoroaster was a dualist. Second, others argue, just as forcefully and as satisfactorily, for the opposite: that Zoroaster was a monotheist. Third, a number of scholars combine the two arguments by suggesting that Zoroaster was both a monotheist and a dualist. And fourth, a few scholars suggest that Zoroaster was neither a monotheist nor a dualist but a prophet who stands at an early stage in a continuum that is to be traced from mythology to philosophy.

To recount the arguments put forward by various critics is tedious and unnecessary. Suffice it to say that the enigmatic nature of the sources permits the proliferation of differing views. Indeed, most of the information we possess seem to fluctuate between dualistic and monotheistic concepts. A few instances will suffice to illustrate this problem.

First, Zoroaster's teachings imply that there is an inherent imbalance of power between two separate primordial forces of good and evil. What is insisted upon in all the sacred texts is the total destruction of the evil principle by the good force; the complete and final triumph of Ahura Mazda to reign supreme; and the end of human history.

Second, the ideas of Zoroaster explain Ahura Mazda's claim to infinite wisdom. The unintelligent (virtually ignorant), deceitful machinations of the rival, evil principle are simply no match for Ahura Mazda's intelligence, forethought, and insight.

Third, Zoroaster's theory on human nature adequately justifies the critical role of human allegiance: the course of human history depends on the choice humans make. But humans possess a "natural responsiveness" to Ahura Mazda's persuasive power, which makes the evil principle's defeat inevitable. This means that human acts, words, and thoughts are decisive in shaping cosmic values.

What then may be concluded from all of this? It seems that Zoroaster tried to reform the ancient Persian polytheistic concept by promoting the supremacy of Ahura Mazda. With Ahura Mazda as the only one, the notions hitherto associated in the ancient Persian cosmology with the other *ahura* and *daeva* became subordinate to Him. And perhaps, without taking all their primitive meaning, Zoroaster made these notions the powers or entities of Ahura Mazda. Furthermore, the elements of struggle that lay scattered in the ancient Persian myths of gods, demons, and monsters Zoroaster welded into a single universal conflict: good versus evil, in which Ahura Mazda and humans took part together. To be sure, the evil principle co-existed with Ahura Mazda, but in no way was it co-equal, co-eternal, or even worthy of worship. In fact, the inevitable outcome was the destruction of the evil principle, the end of human history, the judgment of human beings, the reward and punishment of each individual, and the supreme reign of Ahura Mazda throughout eternity. In other words, Zoroaster's teachings imply that he perceived two distinct ages: this present, temporal, "dualistic age," to be followed by an eternal, "monotheistic age," thanks to the responsive choice of human beings.

5

Baha'u'llah

In the Divine Holy Books (i.e., Torah, Gospels, Qur'an, etc.) there
are unmistakable prophecies giving the Glad Tidings of a certain
Day in which the promised One (i.e., Baha'u'llah) of all the Books
would appear.

(HORACE HOLLEY, ED., *BAHAI SCRIPTURES*, p. 268)

The story of Baha'u'llah (1817–1892) is the story of an individual
whose religion took root in Iran. Almost from the very beginning its
nature and scope was thought to be universal and not restricted to
any particular group. Early in its history, the religious movement,
called Baha'i, embraced on equal terms many converts from
Muslim, Christian, Jewish, and other cultures, who accept the tenets
of the Baha'i faith, recognize the five stations of prophet-hood (The
Bab, Baha'u'llah, Abdul Baha, Shoghi Effendi, and the Universal
House of Justice) and accept the Baha'i scriptures (known as the
Tablets of God), and the Administrative Order.

There are neither paid missionaries nor professional clergy in the
Baha'i religion. All the work of teaching and spreading the faith is
done by volunteers known as pioneers. Much of the work demands
sacrifices from individual believers, who leave their homes, their
careers, and their comforts in order to spread the Baha'i faith. Thus,
the Baha'i faith is one of the youngest religious movements that is
increasingly spreading throughout the world.

Who was Baha'u'llah, and what did he teach? Before answering
those questions it is necessary to present a brief historical background of the world into which Baha'u'llah appeared.

Iran: The Religious World of Baha'u'llah

The Persians, who occupied and settled in the territory of Iran in the course of several centuries and in subsequent waves shortly after 1500 BCE, ruled a vast territory in the Middle East for over a thousand years, from about 550 BCE to 651 CE. All during the Sassanid Persian Empire (224–651 CE) the Persians were engaged in constant conflict with the Roman Empire. In the end, internal strife, assassinations, and rebellions by claimants and counter claimants plagued the Persian throne. And yet, the greatest blow came not from the internal disorder of the Persian Empire but from the Arab conquest of Persia.

The victorious progress of the Arab conquerors was swift and catastrophic. Indeed, the Muslim Arab invasion in the seventh century destroyed the existing Persian political, cultural, and religious forces. Driven by their newly adopted religious fervour and by their craving for power and wealth, the Muslim Arabs became masters of most of Persia. Many Persians adopted Islam either by conversion or coercion. Whatever the case, the Muslim invasion not only arrested the expansion of Zoroastrianism but threatened to annihilate its adherents. Through some unexplained course of events, however, a small group managed to survive the sweeping wave of the Muslim Empire.

The conversion to Islam, however, did not destroy a sense of separate Persian identity. In fact, the majority population of modern Iran speak in Persian. The establishment of Shi'ism (a branch of Islam) as the state religion during the Safavid dynasty (1501–1722) lay the basis for modern Iranian nationalism.[1] There are, however, significant minorities of Sunni and Sufi Muslims, Jews, Christians, Azeris, Assyrians, Baluchis, Kurds, and bands of Turkic speakers.

Shi'i Muslims, particularly in Iran, have always claimed that there are twelve legitimate descendants, or *imams*, of 'Ali, the son-in-law and successor of the Prophet Muhammad.[2] The twelve imams are often referred to as *babs* (gates), because they are believed to function as the gates by which believers gain access to the true faith. Shi'is have always believed that one day the twelfth *imam*, who disappeared under mysterious and unexplained circumstances during the ninth century, would reappear as the Messiah.

In 1844, a Persian Shi'i Muslim, Sayyid 'Ali-Muhammad Shirazi (1819–1850), declared he was the long-awaited twelfth *imam* and assumed the title "The Bab."[3] Gathering around him a group of disciples, who called themselves "Bab'is," The Bab launched a movement for religious and social reform. Within a short time, the movement had gained so much momentum that both religious and political forces in Iran took drastic counteraction. The Bab was publicly executed on July 9, 1850, and many of his followers were eliminated through either imprisonment or execution. Before The Bab died, however, he foretold the appearance of a leader greater than he to carry on the work of establishing a universal religion. Thus his remaining disciples were sustained by the hope that all was not lost. Mirza Husayn-'Ali Nuri (1817–1892), the eldest son of the minister of state, was among the group of survivors. Because of his family connections, he was spared the fate of many of his companions. He had abandoned his family name and assumed the title "Baha'u'llah" (Glory of God).

Traditional Account

Mirza Husayn-'Ali was born in Teheran on 12 November 1817 to a notable landowning family call Nuri, who traced its origin back to the Persian Sassanian kings of Persia. His father, Mirza Abbas Nuri (d. 1839) had four wives and three concubines, by whom he had a total of fifteen children. Baha'u'llah was the third child by the second wife, Khadiji. He married three wives and had a total of eight children.

Baha'u'llah's father was an important government official until he was forced out of office in 1835 by Haji Mirza Aqasi, the chief minister and spiritual adviser of Muhammad Shah of Iran (r.1834–1848). As a young man, Baha'u'llah showed strong religious and mystical tendencies. Evidently he sympathized with some aspects, though not all, of Sufism (Islamic mystical group) and lived the life of a solitary dervish (hermit).[4] Later he joined The Bab movement and helped to spread this new religion among his family and native province. Soon, he assumed a prominent position within the religion and changed his name to Baha.[5]

An event that occurred in 1852 affected the future course of The Bab movement. One of The Bab's followers attempted to assassinate the Iranian Shah, an act that provoked further persecution against the Bab'is (name of followers of The Bab). Baha'u'llah was imprisoned and later exiled to Baghdad, then under the jurisdiction of the Turkish government. During that period, which lasted approximately ten years, a number of significant developments occurred.

First, Baha'u'llah made his place of residence in Baghdad a centre of learning that attracted many students from near and far, and the many Bab'is gradually formed a community in exile. Second, Baha'u'llah wrote several books, including Hidden Words, Seven Valleys, and The Book of Certitude, all aimed at encouraging and guiding his followers. Third, it was revealed to Baha'u'llah that he was the long-awaited leader predicted by The Bab. Fourth, when the authorities in Baghdad sought to suppress The Bab's movement, Baha'u'llah was ordered into even more distant exile – Istanbul (Constantinople) in Turkey.

While the caravan was being prepared for the long journey, Baha'u'llah and his dedicated followers encamped for twelve days (April 21–May 2, 1863) in the garden of Ridvan, just outside Baghdad. When all had assembled, Baha'u'llah made an unexpected announcement: the one whose coming had been foretold by their master, The Bab, was none other than he, Baha'u'llah. All those who recognized him as the Chosen of God, the Promised One of all the prophets, were to follow him.[6] Except for a few who remained unconvinced, the company of Bab'is recognized him as the fulfilment of the prophecy and from that day called themselves Baha'is.

The caravan of displaced Baha'is paused in Istanbul for only a few months before being forced to move on to Adrianople, in European Turkey. During his four and a half years in Adrianople, Baha'u'llah resumed his teaching and gathered a large following. He wrote letters to numerous religious leaders, rulers, and kings, including Queen Victoria, Napoleon Bonaparte III, the Czar of Russia, the Pope, and the president of the United States.[7] To all he announced his mission and called upon them to promote the unity of humanity and the establishment of the true, universal religion.

His energetic proselytizing, however, stimulated further opposition, which resulted in the banishment of Baha'u'llah and his followers to Acre, in Palestine, then a Turkish enclave to which criminals were exiled. A few years later the restrictions that had at first been imposed on the small religious colony were relaxed, and shortly afterward Baha'u'llah and his group moved to Bahji, on the slopes of Mount Carmel, in Israel. His mission, however, terminated with his death on May 29, 1892, at the age of seventy-five. Today, a shrine dedicated to his memory stands on Mount Carmel.

Successors of Baha'u'llah

Before his death, Baha'u'llah made a will in which he appointed his eldest son, 'Abbas Effendi 'Abd al-Baha (1844–1921), his successor and the interpreter of his written works. In assuming leadership of the movement, 'Abbas Effendi changed his name to Abdul Baha ("Servant of Baha," or "Servant of Glory"). He had shared persecutions, exiles, and imprisonment with his father, and now as leader he carried on his father's program of writing. In 1908, when he was freed by the Turkish authorities, he undertook extensive teaching tours in Europe, the United States, and Canada. He preached and taught the Baha'i faith and established numerous assemblies in various nations. Upon his return to Palestine, he wrote The Divine Plan, a work that invoked all Baha'is to spread Baha'u'llah's message – the unification of humankind through the medium of Baha'i – to the four corners of the world. He died on November 28, 1921, at the age of seventy-seven, leaving a will that directed his grandson, Shoghi Effendi Rabbani (1896–1957), to assume leadership of the Baha'i faith. Shoghi Effendi was the last in the direct line of succession from Baha'u'llah. He continued the work of establishing local and national assemblies in various parts of the world until his death on November 2, 1957. Two important innovations were made under his guidance: the structure that governs matters of administration and the Universal House of Justice, which is the supreme legislative body governing the affairs of the Baha'i faith at the international level.

Written Works of Baha'u'llah

The written works of The Bab, Baha'u'llah, Abdul Baha, and Shoghi Effendi, which make up the sacred literature of the Baha'is, are considered to be inspired yet human, poetic yet practical.[8] The writings of Baha'u'llah are comprehensive in range and deal with every phase of human life: individual and social, moral and spiritual. His work also includes prayers, ecstatic poems, visionary accounts of his religious experiences, interpretations of ancient and modern scriptures of other religions, as well as prophetic pronouncements, all written in either Persian or Arabic. Only a small part of his writings has been translated into English. The following is a summary of his better known works.

Among the hundreds of writings of Baha'u'llah, two books are regarded as being especially important by Baha'is: the *Kitab-i-Aqdas* (*Most Holy Book*, composed in Arabic around 1873) and the *Kitab-i-Iqan* (*Book of Certitude*, composed in Persian around 1861). The former deals with Baha'i laws and institutions, and the latter consists of revelatory concepts. Baha'is consider both books no less divinely inspired than the sacred writings of other religions.

Another document that is considered unique by the Baha'i is the *Kitab-i-Ahd* (*Book of the Covenant*, composed in Arabic in 1892). This is considered to be the last will and testament written by Baha'u'llah himself during his final illness, and given to Abdul Baha. The document was read both to a select group of witnesses and to a large gathering of Baha'is nine days after his death. In this will, Baha'u'llah explicitly stipulates the appointment of his eldest son, Abdul Baha, as his successor, and as the only one divinely authorized to interpret his writings.

Teachings of Baha'u'llah

Abdul Baha, as the authorized interpreter of Baha'u'llah's teachings, summarized them in a set of principles. Twelve of the most important of those principles are the following: [9]

1. **Truth.** Truth is one and does not admit of multiple divisions. Each individual must seek the truth independently, forsaking imitations and traditions.

2. **Humanity.** All of the people of the world are created by God and are therefore members of one human family. Because God is just, kind, and merciful to all members of the human race, each individual should follow God's example in dealing with others.

3. **Peace.** The establishment of a permanent and universal peace through world government will be achieved in this century (i.e., twentieth).

4. **Religion and Science.** Humanity is endowed with intelligence and reason to test the validity of ideas. If religious beliefs and opinions fly in the face of scientific evidence, then they are little more than superstitions and unfounded assumptions.

5. **Prejudice.** Prejudice destroys human well-being and happiness; therefore, humanity must actively work to abolish all forms of prejudice – religious, racial, class, and national.

6. **Gender.** Differences that distinguish one gender from the other are not peculiar to humans; those differences are common to all living things and do not favor one sex over the other. Therefore, the equality of men and women must be universally acknowledged.

7. **Economy.** Happiness, prosperity, and the stability of humanity depend on economic equality. Society, therefore, must adjust the balance of the global economy in favor of the majority instead of the few.

8. **Human rights.** God's dominion is characterized by justice and equity without distinction or preference, so a uniform standard of human rights must be universally recognized and adopted.

9. **Education.** Because education is essential to humanity, there should be one universal standard of training and teaching. The universal curriculum also should establish a global code of ethics.

10. **Language.** One of the great factors in the unification of human beings is language. Therefore, a specially appointed committee should select an auxiliary language that will be universally adopted as a medium of international communication.

11. **Work.** Any work performed in a spirit of service is considered to be an act of worship.

12. **Religions.** The universal message of all religions is the same: peace and goodwill. It is in the interest of humanity that all religious systems dispel animosity, bigotry, and hatred and promote love, accordance, and spiritual brotherhood.

An Assessment

The Baha'i faith originated in Iran and is one of the more recent Middle Eastern religions seeking converts throughout the world.[10] Like most other modern religious groups, it has assimilated beliefs and practices from other previous faiths, Eastern and Western, extant and extinct. Chosen prophets or messengers of God include the following: Abraham, Moses, Zoroaster, Krishna, Buddha, Jesus, Muhammad, and Bah'u'llah. In addition, it adumbrates elements of modern science. The integration of religious and scientific ideas on a global scale has been its magnetic appeal to masses in the modern era. Its appeal is due largely to its progressive features, particularly in the areas of reason, science, education, global community, and international languages and government. It denounces prejudices against race, sex, and religion. Its openness to the truth found in all religions, its vision of one world at peace under one government, and its teachings of disarmament have all contributed to its successful spread. Its basic teaching can be summed up in nine words: the oneness of God and the unity of humanity.

The International Headquarters of the faith, known as the World Centre, is located in Haifa, Israel. Unlike other religious organizations, Baha'i institutions are social rather than ecclesiastical. The group's Spiritual Assemblies, both local and national, are responsible for upholding the teachings, conducting the meetings, stimulating active service, and promoting the welfare of the Baha'i cause. Perhaps it is too early to determine whether or not the followers of the Baha'i faith will succeed in establishing a separate and permanent group or movement. Time will tell.

Concluding Observations

Let us hear the conclusion of the whole matter: Fear God and keep
His commandments; for that is the whole duty of man.

(ECCLESIASTES 12:13)

In the preceding pages we surveyed five individuals who claimed to
have received divine messages from God. Fortunately, their
followers recorded their biography otherwise we would have been
unable to know the details of their life and teaching. Even if there
are missing gaps in the writings presented by their biographers, we
still possess enough information to consider their dominant characteristics. So let us review the similarities and differences of those
individuals by considering the following features: biographical
sketch and basic concepts.

Biographical Sketch

According to our sources, all five were born at different times in
different areas of the Middle East: Moses in Egypt, Jesus in Palestine
(modern Israel) under Roman rule, Muhammad in Arabia,
Zoroaster in Persia (modern Iran), and Baha'u'llah in Iran. Their
date of birth cannot be determined exactly; so for the moment let
us accept the calculations proposed by recent scholars: Moses (*ca.*
13th century BCE), Jesus (*ca.* 4 BCE to 29 CE), Muhammad (570 to
632 CE), Zoroaster (*ca.* 14th to 6th century BCE), and Baha'u'llah
(1817–1892 CE). The same kind of difficulty also applies to their
social position in life (prior to their encounter with the divine) as
well as their end of life. The available sources present the following
picture.

Moses, who was the adopted child of Pharaoh's daughter, acted
as liberator, leader, and lawgiver for his own people. In other words,
he rescued his people from Egypt, brought them to the same mountain as that of his own spiritual discovery, and established an eternal

covenant between God and his people. He died without having entered the promised land at the age of 120.

Jesus was widely known as a marvelous wonder worker, so the afflicted came to him seeking relief. Although many followers joined him and went about with him from place to place, twelve of them were chosen as an especially "intimate" circle. Not everybody, however, was pleased with his teaching. His free association with the lowest dregs of society and his lack of interest to many of the accepted requirements of the legal traditions offended the Jewish religious leaders. Consequently they felt that his teaching was subversive. In the end one of his intimate disciples betrayed him to his enemies who after a hasty trial condemned him as a blasphemer, and prevailed on the Roman governor to authorize his execution. To the dismay of his frightened followers Jesus was crucified on the cross at the age of about 33.

Muhammad was a caravan dealer who began to teach what had been revealed to him to individuals of his own family and relatives. Soon others accepted him as God's chosen messenger. His enemies, however, who found Muhammad's family so solidly behind him, decided to boycott against his entire clan. Muhammad himself was too well established to be seriously injured by such persecution, though some of his wealthy followers suffered severely. In a very short time Muhammad successfully united the tribes which constituted the population of Medina and Mecca. As a matter of fact, in a few years Muhammad became the ruler of the entire Arabian Peninsula. He even sent messengers to the rulers of the Persian and Roman Byzantine empires demanding acceptance of his religion. But his health prevented him from undertaking the conquest of these nations when he died from an illness at the age of 62.

Zoroaster was a priest who gained very few followers at first, but after miraculously curing one of the king's horses, the king, the queen, and the royal court adopted his teaching. Other conversions soon followed and Zoroaster's teaching began to spread until his death at the age of 77.

As to Baha'u'llah, in 1868 the Turkish authorities were instrumental in exiling him to Acre in Palestine. At first he was confined to the barracks, but later he moved to a house, and finally to a mansion in the countryside where he remained until his death at the age of 75.

The decisive religious experience which determined the subsequent course of events of those individuals is described in some detail in the respective sacred texts. We shall consider the initial encounter with the divine of five individuals, even though the written records state very explicitly that every one of them had additional divine encounters during their entire lifetime. So, let us start with Moses.

The story of the turning point of Moses occurred after he fled from Egypt for committing the crime of killing an Egyptian. One day when he was herding a flock of sheep near the mountain of Horeb (also known as Mount Sinai), a wondrous site met his eye. The angel of God appeared to him in a flame of fire out of the midst of the bush. Moses looked, and behold the bush was burning, but was not consumed. When Moses drew near to see the marvel more closely, a voice from the burning bush warned him to remove his sandals and stop from coming closer, for the ground on which he stood was holy. Then God spoke to Moses regarding the suffering and tears of His (God's) people who were in Egypt, and charged Moses to return to Pharaoh and demand the release of His people out of Egypt. Reluctant to accept such a responsible mission, Moses raised one objection after another, to which God answered every one of them. Finally, when Moses appealed for his lack of eloquence he was told that his brother Aaron would be his spokesman. Additional encounters with the divine occurred during the entire life of Moses.

The circumstances under which Jesus came to recognize his initial encounter with the divine happened when he was baptized in the Jordan River by John the Baptist. When he came out of the water he saw the heavens opened and the spirit descending upon him like a dove, and a voice from heaven saying, "You are my beloved son, with you I am very pleased." This personal experience marked the turning point in Jesus' life. Immediately following this incident, it is said, Jesus withdrew to a solitary place, the wilderness beyond Jordan, before finally deciding his future career. What actually happened during those forty days in the wilderness is a mystery. One of the writers (Mark 1:13) says simply that Jesus was there for forty days with the wild beasts and that the angels administered him; while two other writers (Matthew 4:3–11; Luke 4:1–12) record that the devil appeared in person and presented three temptations to which Jesus answered each time by saying, "it is written…", referring to the Torah, the Jewish scripture. When the devil finally left him, angels came and ministered to him. Jesus then came out of the wilderness and returned to Galilee, proclaiming the nearness of the kingdom of God, as John the Baptist had done, and calling on the people to repent. He delivered his message in the synagogues, on the seashore, and on country hillsides.

More than five hundred years after the appearance of Jesus another individual claimed to have received a divine call. As a young man, Muhammad often wandered into the hills, especially into a cave outside Mecca, to seek solitude for his meditation. It was on one such visit to the cave that Muhammad heard a divine voice, which said, "Recite!" Overwhelmed by this voice and the appearance of the archangel Gabriel, Muhammad fell prostrate to the ground. The voice repeated, "Recite!" "What shall I recite?" asked Muhammad in terror. And the answer came: "Recite in the name of your Lord who created . . . ." Terrified by the overwhelming divine presence, Muhammad rushed home and told his wife whether to regard it as a sign of mental disorder or to accept it as a genuine revelation. His wife tried to calm and comfort him, but it was long before he overcame the haunting fear that he might be mad. Finally, the genuineness of the divine encounter emboldened Muhammad to trust additional revelations, and he began to teach what was given to him.

One day when Zoroaster was carrying the sacred water, he was met by an archangel who asked him what his uppermost desire was. Zoroaster's reply was that his greatest desire was to devote himself to God and prepare for the coming of God's kingdom. On hearing Zoroaster's reply, the archangel brought him into the presence of God. This vision constituted Zoroaster's call to be a prophet. Tradition states, furthermore, that during the following ten years Zoroaster had six additional divine encounters.

As to Baha'u'llah, one day while he and his followers were in the garden of Ridvan (outside Baghdad) he announced to the assembled that the one whose coming had been foretold by the Bab was none other than he. All those who recognized him as the chosen of God, the promised one of all the prophets, were to follow him.

Basic Concepts

It is extremely difficult, if not impossible, to present a picture that will fully satisfy every one. Surely one must realize that our information derives from what has been preserved in the principal sources. And yet it is very difficult to separate the basic concepts and teachings of the founders of religion from the additional assumptions or speculations contributed by the writers and editors. The endeavor to identify both has not been altogether fortunate. Not to mention the bitter strife that has often divided the community of believers into hostile camps. Furthermore, we must recognize that every new religious movement grows out of an older one, either as a further development or as a revolt.

Be that as it may, we now need to consider the following questions: What were the basic teachings of those five selected messengers? Do their messages have something in common or do they differ? In what way did their message differ from traditional beliefs and customs?

It is not easy, at first sight, to detect any unity at all among the five who lived at different times and geographical territories of the Middle East. The differences cannot be ignored because they are as real and as important as the similarities. One fundamental assumption, however, seems to underlie all of them: a personal divine encounter! This personal experience with the divine, a "call" or "voice" directly from the "beyond," seems to have been shared by all five: Moses and the "voice" from the burning bush, Zoroaster and the "voice" by the Daiti River, Jesus and the "voice" by the Jordan River, Muhammad and the "voice" in the cave outside Mecca, and Baha'u'llah at the garden of Ridvan just outside Baghdad. The importance of this basic agreement can hardly be exaggerated.

Equally important, though not fully in accord, is the concept of monotheism – the belief in a personal God. Moses, to be sure, was not strictly a monotheist, because (most probably) he did not question the existence of other gods. He did insist, however, on the exclusive worship of YHWH, the God of the Fathers (*avot*). Jewish and Christian scholars may disagree on this viewpoint. But as most scholars know, the question of who was the "first" real monotheist has never been satisfactorily resolved. The three disputed figures are Akhenaton, Moses, and Zoroaster. The difficulty lies in the surviving literature, the inscriptional evidence, and the archaeological discoveries. Consequently, the available sources of information provide conflicting images of those three.

The question, therefore, of who was "first" to suggest the idea of monotheism is a most perplexing matter among scholars. What we know is that the conception of the universe shared by almost all the peoples of the Middle East regarded the gods and goddesses to be "immanent" in nature; and this rendered the universe as well as creatures with divinity. Diametrically opposed to this polytheistic view is the monotheistic conception of the selected messengers: the existence of one "transcendent" God, who is outside and above all nature which He created. The position of human beings is similar: their origin and destiny derive from God. Thus, all five demonstrate great originality by braking sharply with the polytheistic religious traditions of the Middle East.

There are, however, differences that must not be ignored. They are as real and as important as the similarities. Here, as elsewhere, the influence of inherited conceptions is evident. This means that each messenger, whether he adopts or rejects the prevailing views of his day, remains distinctly and characteristically Persian/Iranian, Jew, or Arab, as the case may be.

With monotheism go omniscience, omnipotence, and omnipresence. Muhammad lays more stress upon these attributes of God than Moses, Jesus and Zoroaster do, though all three of them regard God as the creator and ruler of all. Again, we find a great diversity of ideas among the five regarding the following four important issues: Devil (Satan, Adversary), God's kingdom, life after death, and eternal judgment. Three of the five messengers, Zoroaster, Jesus, and Muhammad, seem to acknowledge the existence of the devil, look forward to the complete and final triumph of God's kingdom, and anticipate bodily resurrection and eternal judgment of heaven or hell.[1] Moses had nothing to say to this effect. In Judaism those beliefs developed long after the time of Moses, probably in the exilic period through Zoroastrian influence. It must be remembered, however, that Moses differed from the others in one fundamental point: he saved his people from total extinction.

Perhaps the most far reaching difference between the founders is in their approach or outlook toward social institutions such as position of women, marriage, polygamy, divorce, law, war, morality, ethics, government, and so on. No single, dominating principle is evident among the selected messengers. Through all the confusing variety of ideals and conceptions there are a few points that stand out as of primary importance.

Moses and Muhammad are both administrators and legislators. The value of good government is stressed by Zoroaster. Laws revealed from heaven are taught by Moses and Muhammad. Jesus defines righteousness in terms of obedience to the Law. Both Zoroaster and Muhammad regard war as worthy and useful for the propagation of truth. Active participation on the right side of the cosmic struggle is Zoroaster's basic principle.

These few examples are sufficient to demonstrate that the ideas of what constitutes right or proper living differ among the selected messengers. In fact, their diverse ideas or points of view make all the more significant the things they held in common. Few as these are, they are of the utmost importance.

Notes

Introduction

1 For an introduction to the ancient Near East, including its societies, political systems, historical problems, and scholarly debates, consult Kuhrt, *The Ancient Near East c. 3000–330 BC*; Van de Mieroop, *A History of the Ancient Near East (ca. 3000–323 BC)*; for the social and economic history of the ancient Near East see Snell, *Life in the Ancient Near East 3100–332 BCE*; for an archaeological presentation of the early history of the ancient Near East see Finkelstein, *Living on the Fringe: The Archaeology and History of the Negev, Sinai and Neighbouring Regions in the Bronze and Iron Ages*; Nissen, *The Early History of the Ancient Near East 9000–2000 BC*.

2 On Persia, consult the following books: Briant, *From Cyrus to Alexander: A History of the Persian Empire*; Cook, *The Persian Empire*.

3 James B. Pritchard, ed. *The Ancient Near East: An Anthology of Texts and Pictures*, vol.1, pp. 315–316.

4 On Alexander the Great see Bosworth, *Conquest and Empire: The Reign of Alexander the Great*.

5 On the Romans see McLaren, *Power and Politics in Palestine: The Jews and The Governing of Their Land*; Kamm, *The Romans: An Introduction*.

6 Cited in Henry Bettenson, ed. *Documents of the Christian Church*, 2nd ed. London: Oxford University Press, pp. 15–16.

7 Theodosian Code XVI.10.25 (435) in *The Theodosian Code and Novels and Sirmondian Constitutions*. Princeton, NJ.: Princeton University Press, 1952, p. 476.

8 On Mani and Manichaeism, see Nicholas J. Baker-Brian, *Manichaeism: An Ancient Faith Recovered*; J.D. BeDuhn, *The Manichaean Body in Discipline and Ritual*; Ian Gardner and Samuel N.C. Lieu, eds., *Manichaean Texts from the Roman Empire*; Samuel N.C. Lieu, *Manichaeism in Mesopotamia and the Roman East*; Samuel N.C. Lieu, *Manichaeism in the Later Roman Empire and Medieval China*; J. Van Oort, *Mani, Manichaeism and Augustine: The Rediscovery of Manichaeism and Its Influence on Western Christianity*; H.C. Puech, *Le manichéisme: son fondateur, sa doctrine*; Michel Tardieu, *Manichaeism*; G. Widengren, *Mani and Manichaeism*.

Chapter 1 Moses

1 There are lots of books on Egypt; among others, see, Chadwick, *First Civilizations: Ancient Mesopotamia and Ancient Egypt*; Rosalie, *The Experience of Ancient Egypt*; Shaw, *Ancient Egypt: A Very Short Introduction*.

2 Dodson, *The Pyramids of Ancient Egypt*; Gibbons, *Mummies, Pyramids, and Pharaohs: A Book about Ancient Egypt*.

3 On Egyptian gods and goddesses see, Meeks and Meeks. *Daily Life of the Egyptian Gods*; Morenz, *Egyptian Religion*; Redford, *The Ancient Gods Speak: A Guide to Egyptian Religion*.

4 See Germond and Livet, *An Egyptian Bestiary: Animals in Life and Religion in the Land of The Pharaohs*.

5 On Egyptian priests see Sauneron, *The Priests of Ancient Egypt*.

6 Colt, *Isis and Osiris: Exploring the Goddess Myth*.

7 Gibbons, *Mummies, Pyramids, and Pharaohs: A Book About Ancient Egypt*.

8 Taylor, *Death and the Afterlife in Ancient Egypt*; Allen, *The Book of the Dead, or Going Forth by Day*.

9 Ions, *Egyptian Mythology*.

10 Montserrat, *Akhenaten: History, Fantasy, and Ancient Egypt*; Redford, *Akhenaten: The Heretic King*.

11 The figure of Moses as presented in the Jewish scripture has intrigued modern scholars; see, among others, the works of the following listed in the bibliography: Assmann, Beegle, Coats, Nigosian, van Seeters.

12 See Nigosian, *From Ancient Writings to Sacred Texts: The Old Testament and Apocrypha*, chs. 1–2.

13 The following discussion is adapted from Nigosian, "Moses as They Saw Him," pp. 339–50.

14 See Nigosian, "The Song of Moses (DT 32): A Structural Analysis," pp. 5–22.

15 Hinnells, *Who's Who of World Religions*, p. 277.

Chapter 2 Jesus

1 For Palestine at the time of Jesus see Hanson, *Palestine in the Time of Jesus: Social Structures and Social Conflicts*; for an introduction on the history of Rome see Cary and Scullard, *A History of Rome Down to the Reign of Constantine*; for the Jews at that time see Russell, *The Jews from Alexander to Herod*.

2 See, Ando, *Roman Religion*; North, *Roman Religion*; Scheid, *An Introduction to Roman Religion*.

3 Vermaseren, *Cybele and Attis: The Myth and the Cult*.

4 On Isis-Serapis see Takacs, *Isis and Sarapis in the Roman World*.

5 Clauss, *The Roman Cult of Mithras: The God and His Mysteries*; Cooper, *Mithras: Mysteries and Initiation Rediscovered*.

6 Gradel, *Emperor Worship and Roman Religion*.

7 Stemberger, *Jewish Contemporaries of Jesus: Pharisees, Sadducees, Essenes*.

8 Biblical scholars differ in many details regarding the collection of the four Gospels; see, among others, Funk, *New Gospel Parallels*; Funk, *The Gospel of Jesus: According to the Jesus Seminar*; Funk, *The Once and Future Jesus: The Jesus Seminar*; Kloppenborg, *Q Parallels: Synopsis, Critical Notes, and Concordance*; Sanders, and Davies. *Studying the Synoptic Gospels*; Shin, *Textual Criticism and the Synoptic Problem in Historical Jesus Research: The Search for Valid Criteria*; Sanders, *Jesus and Judaism*; Stanton, *The Gospels and Jesus*.

9 Scholarly works on Jesus are plenty; among others, see, Crossan, *Jesus: A Revolutionary Biography*; Crotty, *The Jesus Question: The Historical Search*; Herzog, *Prophet and Teacher: An Introduction to the Historical Jesus*; Stanton, *The Gospels and Jesus*; Theissen, *The Historical Jesus: A Comprehensive Guide*; Weaver, *Jesus and His Biographers*; White, *From Jesus to Christianity*.

Chapter 3 Muhammad

1 Various sections of this chapter have been adapted from my book, Nigosian, *Islam*.

2 On the history of the Arabs see, among others, Hourani, *A History of The Arab Peoples*; Hoyland, *Arabia and the Arabs*; Lewis, *The Arabs in History*; Masfield, *The Arabs*; Rodinson, *The Arabs*.

3 There are numerous books on Muhammad; see among others, Armstrong, *Muhammad: A Biography of the Prophet*; Cook, *Muhammad*; Glubb, *The Life and Times of Muhammad*; Lings, *Muhammad: His Life Based on the Earliest Sources*.

4 For the Qur'an see, Nigosian, *Islam: Its History, Teaching, and Practices*, ch. 4.

5 Watt, *Muhammad: Prophet and Statesman*.

6 For a discussion of the role of Muhammad in popular Muslim piety see, Schimmel, *And Muhammad is His Messenger: The Veneration of the Prophet in Islamic Piety*.

Chapter 4 Zoroaster

1 For Aryans see, Maasson and Sarianidi, *Central Asia: Turkmenia Before the Achaemenids*.

2 For Persians see, Allen, *The Persian Empire*; Kuhrt, *The Persian Empire*, 2 vols.

3 For the Magi see, Yamauchi, *Persia and the Bible*, pp. 467–91.

4 For the traditional account of Zoroaster see, Nigosian, *The Zoroastrian Faith*, pp. 11–14; also Boyce, *A History of Zoroastrianism*.
5 For the Zoroastrian scriptures see Nigosian, *The Zoroastrian Faith*, pp. 46–70.
6 The following discussion is adapted from Nigosian, *The Zoroastrian Faith*, pp.14–24. For a survey of divergent scholarly theories see Gnoli, *Zoroaster's Time and Homeland*; Hartman, *Parsiism, The Religion of Zoroaster*; Henning, *Zoroaster, Politician or Witch-Doctor?*

Chapter 5 Baha'u'llah

1 On Iran, see Bausani, *Religion in Iran: From Zoroaster to Baha'u'llah*; Fischer, *Iran: From Religious Dispute to Revolution*.
2 On the Shi'i Muslims, see Momen, *An Introduction to Shi'i Islam: The History and Doctrines of Twelver Shi'ism*.
3 On the Bab, see Bab, *Selections from the Writings of the Bab*; H. M. Balyuzi, *The Bab*; D. MacEoin, *Early Babi Doctrine and History*; M. Momen, *The Babi and Baha'i Religions: Some Contemporary Western Accounts*.
4 On mysticism in Islam, see Baldick, *Mystical Islam: An Introduction to Sufism*; Bayat, *Mysticism and Dissent: Socioreligious Thought in Qajar Iran*.
5 R.M. Afnan, *The Revelation of Baha'u'llah and the Baba*.
6 On Baha'u'llah, see H. M. Balyuzi, *Baha'u'llah: The King of* Glory; John E. Esselmont, *Baha'u'llah and the New Era*; Hofman, *Baha'u'llah, The Prince of Peace: A Portrait*.
7 For the letters written by Baha'u'llah to world rulers, religious leaders, and other individuals, see Holley, ed., *Bahai Scriptures*, chapter 2, pp. 67–136.
8 Works written by Baha'u'llah and his successors are numerous; among others, see Baha'u'llah, *The Kitab-i-Aqdas; The Hidden Words of Baha'u'llah*; *Gleanings from the Writings of Baha'u'llah*; *Kitab-i-Iqan: The Book of Certitude*; 'Abd al-Baha' *Selections from the Writings of 'Abdul Baha*.
9 Summarized from Holley, ed., *Bahai Scriptures*, pp. 276–279.
10 On the Baha'i faith, see, among others, Bowers, *God Speaks Again: An Introduction to the Bahá'í Faith*; Danesh and Fazel, *Search for Values: Ethics in Bahá'í Thought*; William S. Hatcher, *The Baha'i Faith: The Emerging Global Religion*; McMullen, *The Baha'i: The Religious Construction of a Global Identity*.

Concluding Observations

1 On unity and diversity of ideas in world religions see, S.A. Nigosian, *World Religions: A Historical Approch*, 4th ed., pp. 506–515.

Bibliography

Abbott, Nabia. *Aishah, the Beloved of Mohammed*. Chicago, IL: University Press, 1942; New York: Arno Press, 1973.

'Abd al-Baha' *Selections from the Writings of 'Abdul Baha*, trans. Marzieh Gail. Haifa: Baha'i World Centre, 1978.

Afnan, R.M. *The Revelation of Baha'u'llah and the Baba*. New York: Philosophical Library, 1970.

Allen, Lindsay. *The Persian Empire*. Chicago, IL: University of Chicago Press, 2005.

Allen, Thomas George trans. *The Book of the Dead, or Going Forth by Day*. Chicago, IL: Chicago University Press, 1974.

Ando, Clifford, ed. *Roman Religion*. Edinburgh: Edinburgh University Press, 2003.

Andrae, Tor. *Mohammed, The Man and His Faith*, translated by Theophil Menzel. New York: Harper, 1971.

Antes, Peter, Armin W. Greetz, and Randi R. Warne, eds. *New Approaches to the Study of Religion*. Berlin and New York: Walter de Gruyter, 2004.

Arberry, Arthur John. *Sufism: An Account of the Mystics of Islam*. New York: Harper Torchbooks, 1970.

Arjomand, Said Amir. ed. *Authority and Political Culture in Shi'ism*. Albany, NY: SUNY Press, 1988.

Armstrong, Karen. *Muhammad: A Biography of the Prophet*. New York: HarperCollins, 1992.

Assman, Jan. *The Search for God in Ancient Egypt*, translated by David Lorton. Ithaca, NY: Cornell University Press, 2001.

_____. *Moses the Egyptian: The Memory of Egypt in Western Monotheism*. Cambridge, MA: Harvard University Press, 1997.

Auld, A. Graeme. Joshua, *Moses and the Land: Tetrateuch-Pentateuch-Hexateuch in a Generation Since 1938*. Edinburgh: T&T Clark, 1980.

Averbeck, Richard E., Mark W. Chavalas, and David B. Wiseberg, eds. *Life and Culture in The Ancient Near East*. Potomac, MD: CDL Press, 2003.

Bab. *Selections From the Writings of the Bab*, trans. M. Taherzadeh. Haifa: Baha'i World Centre, 1976.

Badiee, Julie. *An Earthly Paradise: Baha'i Houses of Worship Around the World*. Oxford: G. Ronald, 1992.

Baha'u'llah. *The Hidden Words of Baha'u'llah*, trans. Shoghi Effendi. London: Baha'i Publishing Trust, 1929, 1975.

Baha'u'llah. *Gleanings from the Writings of Baha'u'llah* ed. and trans. Shoghi Effendi. Rev. edn. Willmette, IL: Baha'i Publishing Trust, 1976.

Baha'u'llah. *Kitab-i-Iqan: The Book of Ceritude*, trans. Shoghi Effendi. London: Baha'i Publishing Trust, 1946, 1982.

Baha'u'llah. *The Kitab-i-Aqdas. The Most Holy Book*. London: Baha'i Publishing House, 1993.

Baker-Brian, Nicholas J. *Manichaeism: An Ancient Faith* Recovered London: T&T Clark, 2011.

Baldick, Julian. *Mystical Islam: An Introduction to Sufism*. New York: New York University Press, 1989.

Balyuzi, H. M. *Baha'u'llah: The King of Glory*. Oxford: George Ronald, 1980.

Balyuzi, H. M. *The Bab*. Oxford: Goerge Ronald, 1975.

Balyuzi, H. M. *'Abdu'l Baha: The Centre of the Covenant of Baha'u'llah*. London: George Ronald, 1971.

Bausani, Alessandro. *Religion in Iran: From Zoroaster to Baha'u'llah*. Translated by J.M. Marchesi. New York: Bibliotheca Persica Press; Winona Lake, IN: Distributed by Eisenbrauns, Inc., 2000.

Bayat, Mangol. *Mysticism and Dissent: Socioreligious Thought in Qajar Iran*. Syracuse, NY: Syracuse University Press, 1982.

BeDuhn, Jason David. *The Manichaean Body in Discipline and Ritual*. Baltimore/Londom: The Johns Hopkins University Press, 2000.

Beegle, Dewey M. *Moses, The Servant of Yahweh*. Ann Arbor, MI: Pryor Pettengill, 1979.

Bosworth, A. B. *Conquest and Empire: The Reign of Alexander the Great*. New York: Cambridge University Press, 1988.

Bowers, Kenneth E. *God Speaks Again: An Introduction to the Bahá'í Faith*. Wilmette, IL: Bahá'í Pub., 2004.

Boyce, Mary. *A History of Zoroastrianism*, 3 vols. Leiden: E. J. Brill, 1975–1991.

Briant, Pierre. *From Cyrus to Alexander: A History of the Persian Empire*. trs. by Peter T. Daniels. Winona Lake, IN: Eisenbraun, 2002.

Buber, Martin. *Moses: The Revelation and the Covenant*. Atlantic Highlands, NJ: Humanities Press International, 1988 (original London, 1947).

Burch, G. B. *Alternative Goals in Religion*. Montreal, Canada: McGill–Queen's University Press, 1972.

Campbell, Joseph. *The Power of Myth*. New York: Doubleday, 1988.

Carpenter, Humphrey. *Jesus*. Oxford: Oxford University Press, 1980.

Carter, Robert E., ed. *God, The Self, and Nothingness Reflections: Eastern and Western*. New York: Paragon House, 1990.

Cary, M. and H. H. Scullard. *A History of Rome Down to the Reign of Constantine.* 3rd ed. New York: St. Martin's Press, 1976.

Chadwick, Robert. *First Civilizations: Ancient Mesopotamia and Ancient Egypt.* 2nd ed. Oakville, CT: Equinox Pub. 2004.

Choudhury, G. W. *The Prophet Muhammad: His Life and Eternal Message.* London: Scorpion, 1993.

Clark, Gillian. *Christianity and Roman Society.* Cambridge, MA: Cambridge University Press, 2004.

Clauss, Manfred. *The Roman Cult of Mithras: The God and His Mysteries.* Translated by Richard Gordon. Edinburgh: Edinburgh University Press, 2000.

Coats, George W. *Moses: Heroic Man, Man of God.* JSOTSup 57. Sheffield: JSOT Press, 1988.

_____. *The Moses Tradition.* JSOTSup 161. Sheffield: Sheffield Academic Press, 1993.

Cole, Juan R. I. & Nikkie R. Keddie, eds. *Shi'ism and Social Protest.* New Haven, CT: Yale University Press, 1986.

Colt, Jonathan. *Isis and Osiris: Exploring the Goddess Myth.* New York: Doubleday, 1994.

Connolly, Peter, ed. *Approaches to the Study of Religion.* London and New York: Cassell, 1999.

Cook, John Manuel. *The Persian Empire.* New York: Schocken Books 1983.

Cook, Michael A. *Muhammad.* Oxford: Oxford University Press, 1983.

Cooper, D. Jason. *Mithras: Mysteries and Initiation Rediscovered.* York Beach, ME: S. Weiser, 1996.

Coulmas, Florian. *The Writing Systems of the World.* Oxford: Basil Blackwell, 1991.

Crossan, John D. *Jesus: A Revolutionary Biography.* San Francisco, CA: HarperCollins, 1994.

Crotty, Robert B. *The Jesus Question: The Historical Search.* North Balckburn, Victoria, Australia: HarperCollins Religious, 1996.

Danesh, John and Seena Fazel, eds. *Search for Values: Ethics in Bahá'í Thought.* (Studies in the Bábí and Bahá'í religions, vol. 15). Los Angeles, CA: Kalimat Press, 2004.

Daniels, Peter T. and William Bright, eds. *The World's Writing Systems.* New York, NY: Oxford University Press, Inc. 1996.

David, Ann Rosalie. *The Experience of Ancient Egypt.* London and New York: Routledge, 2000.

Deal, William E., and Timothy K. Beal. *Theory for Religious Studies.* New York: Routledge, 2004.

De Jong, Albert. *Tradition of the Magi: Zoroastrianism in Greek and Latin Literature.* Religions in the Greco-Roman World, vol. 133. Leiden/New York: Brill, 1997.

Dever, William G. *What Did the Biblical Writers Know, and When Did They Know It?: What Archaeology Can Tell Us About the Reality of Ancient Israel.* Grand Rapids, MI: Eerdmans, 2001.

_____. *Who Were the Early Israelites, and Where Did They Come From?* Grand Rapids. MI: Eerdmans, 2003.

Dion, Paul. "YHWH as Storm-god and Sun-god: The Double Legacy of Egypt and Canaan as Reflected in Psalm 104." *ZAW* 103, no. 1 (1991): 43–71.

Dodson, Aidan. *The Pyramids of Ancient Egypt.* London: New Holland, 2003.

Donaldson, Terry. *Paul and the Gentiles: Remapping the Apostle's Convictional World.* Minneapolis, MN: Fortress Press, 1997.

Driver, Godfrey Rolles. *Semitic Writing From Pictograph to Alphabet*, rev. edn. ed. S. A. Hopkins. London: Oxford University Press, 1976.

Dubuisson, Daniel. *The Western Construction of Religion: Myths, Knowledge, and Ideology.* Translated by William Sayers. Baltimore, MD: Johns Hopkins University Press, 2003.

Eliade, Mircae. *The Sacred and the Profane: The Nature of Religion.* New York: Harper & Row, 1961.

_____. *Myths, Dreams and Mysteries.* London: Harvill Press, 1960.

_____. *Myth and Reality.* New York: Harper & Row, 1963.

Esslemont, John Ebenezer. *Baha'u'llah and the New Era.* Wilmette, IL: Baha'i Books, 1976.

Ferguson, J. *The Religions of the Roman Empire.* London: Thames and Hudson, 1970.

Finkelstein, Israel. *Living on the Fringe: The Archaeology and History of the Negev, Sinai and Neighbouring Regions in the Bronze and Iron Ages.* Sheffield: Sheffield Academic Press, 1995.

Firestone, Reuven. *Journeys in Holy Lands: The Evolution of Abraham-Ishmael Legends in Islamic Exegesis.* Albany, NY: SUNY Press, 1990.

Fischer, Michael M.J. *Iran: From Religious Dispute to Revolution.* Cambridge, MA: Harvard University Press, 1980.

Flood, Gavin D. *Beyond Phenomenology: Rethinking the Study of Religion.* London and New York: Cassell, 1999.

Franzmann, Majella. *Jesus in the Manichaean Writings.* London: T&T Clark, 2003.

Frazer, James G. *The Golden Bough: A Study in Magic and Religion*, 3 vols. London: Macmillan, 1900.

Freedman, David Noel, and Michael J. McClymond, eds. *The Rivers of Paradise.* Grand Rapids, MI/Cambridge, UK: William B. Erdmans Publishing Co., 2001.

Freud, Sigmund. *Totem and Taboo.* New York: Moffat, Yard, 1918.

_____ *The Future of an Illusion* .London: Hogarth Press, 1928.

_____ *Civilization and Its Discontents.* London: Hogarth Press, 1930.

Freyne, Seán. *Jesus, A Jewish Galilean: A New Reading of the Jesus Story.* London: T&T Clark, 2004.

Friedman, Saul S. *A History of the Middle East.* Jefferson, NC: McFarland & Co., 2006.

Frye, Richard Nelson. *The History of Ancient Iran.* Munchen: C. H. Beck, 1984.

Funk, Robert Walter. *New Gospel Parallels.* Sonoma, CA: Polebridge Press, 1990.

_____, ed., *The Gospel of Jesus: According to the Jesus Seminar.* Santa Rosa, CA.: Polebridge Press, 1999.

_____, ed., *The Once and Future Jesus: The Jesus Seminar.* Santa Rosa, CA: Polebridge Press, 2000.

Galanter, Marc. *Cults: Faith, Healing, and Coercion.* London and New York: Oxford University Press, 1989.

Gelvin, James L. *The Modern Middle East: A History.* 3rd ed. Oxford, NY: Oxford University Press, 2011.

Germond, Philippe and Jacques Livet. *An Egyptian Bestiary: Animals in Life and Religion in The Land of the Pharaohs.* Translated by Barbara Metpor. London: Thames & Hudson, 2001.

Gibbons, Gail. *Mummies, Pyramids, and Pharaohs: A Book about Ancient Egypt.* New York: Little, Brown, 2004.

Glubb, John Bagot. *The Life And Times of Muhammad.* London: Hodder and Stoughton, 1979.

Goldschmidt, Arthus. *A Concise History of the Middle East.* 10th ed. Boulder, CO: Westview Press 2013.

Gnoli, Gherardo. *Zoroaster's Time And Homeland.* Seminario di Studi Asiatici, Series Minor, Vol. 7. Naples: Istituto Universitario Orientale 1980.

Gothóni, René. *How to Do Comparative Religion?: Three Ways, Many Goals.* Berlin and New York: Walter de Gruyter, 2006.

Gradel, Ittai. *Emperor Worship and Roman Religion.* Oxford: Oxford University Press, 2004.

Gwynne, Paul. *Buddha, Jesus and Muhammad: A Comparative Study.* Malden, MA: Wiley Blackwell, 2014.

Hanson, Kenneth C. *Palestine in the Time of Jesus: Social Structures and Social Conflicts,* 2nd ed. Minneapolis, MN: Fortress Press, 2008.

Harrison, Gordon. *Allah, Jesus, and Yahweh: The Gods That Failed.* Amherst, NY: Prometheus Publications, 2013.

Hartman, Sven S. *Parsiism, The Religion of Zoroaster.* Leiden, The Netherlands: E.J. Brill, 1980.

Hatcher, William S. *The Baha'i Faith: The Emerging Global Religion.* San Francisco: Harper & Row, 1985.

Henning, Walter B. *Zoroaster, Politician or Witch-Doctor?* Oxford: Oxford University Press 1951.

Herzfeld, Ernest. *Zoroaster and His World*, 2 vols. Princeton: Princeton University Press 1947; reprint Octagon Books 1974.

Herzog, William R. *Prophet and Teacher: An Introduction to the Historical Jesus*. Louisville, KY: Westminster John Knox Press, 2005.

Hinnells, J. R. ed. *Who's Who of World Religions*. London: Simon & Schuster, 1992, p. 277.

Hofman, David. *Baha'u'llah, The Prince of Peace: A Portrait*. Oxford: G. Ronald, 1992.

Holley, Horace, ed. *Bahai Scriptures: Selections from the Utterances of Baha'u'llah and Abdul Baha*. New York: Brentano's Publishers, 1923.

Hourani, Albert Habib. *A History of the Arab Peoples*. London: Faber & Faber 1991.

Hoyland, Robert G. *Arabia and the Arabs: From the Bronze Age to the Coming of Islam*. London/New York: Routledge, 2001.

Humphreys, Colin J. *The Miracles of Exodus: A Scientist's Discovery of the Extraordinary Natural Causes of the Biblical Stories*. New York: HarperCollins, 2003.

Ions, Veronica. *Egyptian Mythology*. New York: P. Bedrick Books, 1988.

Jackson, A.V. Williams. *Zoroaster, The Prophet of Ancient Iran*. New York: Macmillan 1899; reprint AMS Press 1965.

Jeffers, Ann. *Magic and Divination in Ancient Palestine and Syria*. Leiden: E. J. Brill, 1996.

Jelen, Ted. G. *Religion and Politics in Comparative Perspective: The One, the Few, and the Many*. Cambridge, MA: Cambridge University Press, 2002.

Jordan, L.H. *Comparative Religion: Its Genesis and Growth*. Edinburgh: T&T Clark, 1905.

Kamm, Anthony. *The Romans: An Introduction*. London/New York: Routledge, 1995.

Kellens, J. *Zoroastre et l'Avesta ancien*. Paris: Université de Sorbonne Nouvelle, 1991.

Kloppenborg, S. *Q Parallels: Synopsis, Critical Notes, and Concordance*. Sonoma, CA: Polebridge Press, 1988.

Kuhrt, Amelie. *The Ancient Near East c. 3000–330 BC*, 2 vols. London/New York: Routledge, 1995.

_____. *The Persian Empire*, 2 vols. London/New York: Routledge, 2007.

Lewis, Bernard. *The Arabs in History*. New York: Harper & Row, 1966.

Lings, Martin. *Muhammad: His Life Based on the Earliest Sources*. Rochester, VT: Inner Traditions, 1983.

_____. *What is Sufism?* Berkley, CA: University of California Press, 1977.

Luz, Ulrich & Axel Michaels. *Encountering Jesus and Buddha: Their Lives and Teachings,* trans by Linda M. Maloney. Minneapolis, MN: Fortress Press, 2006.

MacEoin, D. *Early Babi Doctrine and History*. Los Angeles: Kalimat Press, 1992.

Martin, J. Douglas and William S. Hatcher. *The Baha'i Faith: The Emerging Global Religion*. New York: Harper & Row, 1985.

Marx, Karl. *Capital*, vol. 1, 1867, translated by Samuel Moore and Edward Aveling, edited by F. Engels. London: Lawrence and Wishart, 1961.

Masfield, Peter. *The Arabs*, 3rd ed. London: Penguin, 1985.

Masson, Vadim M. and V.I. Sarianidi. *Central Asia, Turkmenia Before the Achaemenids*. London: Thames & Hudson, 1972

Matsushima, Eiko, ed. *Official Cult and Popular Religion in the Ancient Near East*. Heidelberg: Universitätsverlag C. Winter, 1993.

McLaren, James S. *Power and Politics in Palestine: The Jews and the Governing of Their Land*. Sheffield, UK: JSOTS Press, 1991.

McCutcheon, Russell T. *The Discipline of Religion: Structure, Meaning, Rhetoric*. London and New York: Routledge, 2003.

McMullen, Michael. *The Baha'i: The Religious Construction of a Global Identity*. New Brunswick, NJ: Rutgers University Press, 2000.

Meeks, Dimitri, and Christine Favard Meeks. *Daily Life of the Egyptian Gods*. Trans. by G. M. Goshgarian. Ithaca, NY: Cornell University Press, 1996.

Mehr, Farhang. *The Zoroastrian Tradition: An Introduction to the Ancient Wisdom of Zarathustra*, 2nd ed. Costa Mesa, CA: Mazda, 2003 (Element Inc. 1991).

Miller, William McElwee. *The Baha'i Faith: Its History and Teachings*. Pasadena, CA: Carey Library, 1974.

Momen, Moojan. *An Introduction to Shi' Islam: The History and Doctrines of Twelver Shi'ism*. New Haven, CT: Yale University Press, 1985.

_____. *Islam and the Baha'i Faith*. Oxford: George Ronald, 2000.

Montefiore, Hugh. *The Miracles of Jesus*. London: SPCK, 2005.

Montserrat, Dominic. *Akhenaten: History, Fantasy, and Ancient Egypt*. London/New York: Routledge, 2000.

Morenz, Siegfried. *Egyptian Religion*. London: Methuen, 1973.

Motzki, Harald, ed. *The Biography of Muhammad: The Issue of the Sources*. Islamic History and Civilization: Studies and Text, vol. 32. Leiden, The Netherlands: Brill, 2000.

Müller, Friedrich Max, ed. *The Sacred Books of the East*, 50 vols. Oxford: Clarendon Press, 1879–1910.

_____. *Introduction to the Science of Religion*. London: Longmans, Green, and Co., 1873.

Neville, Robert C. *Behind the Masks of God: An Essay Toward Comparative Theology*. Albany, NY: SUNY, 1991.

Nigosian, Solomon A. *World Religions: A Historical Perspective*, 4th ed. Boston/New York: Bedford/St. Martin's, 2008.

_____. *From Ancient Writings to Sacred Texts: The Old Testament and Apocrypha*. Baltimore, MD: The Johns Hopkins University Press, 2004.

_____. *Islam: Its History, Teaching, and Practices*. Bloomington, IN: Indiana University Press, 2004.

_____. "Linguistic Patterns of Deuteronomy 32." *Biblica* 78, no. 2 (1997): 206–24.

_____. "Moses As They Saw Him." *VT* 43, no. 3 (1993): 339–50.

_____. "The Song of Moses (DT 32): A Structural Analysis." *ETL* 1 (1996): 5–22.

_____. "The Religions in Achaemenid Persia." *Studies in Religion* 4/4 (1974–5): 378–86.

_____. *The Zoroastrian Faith. Tradition and Modern Research*. Montreal, Canada: McGill–Queen's University Press, 1993.

Nissen, Hans J. *The Early History of the Ancient Near East 9000–2000 BC*, translated by Elizabeth Lutzeier, with Kenneth J. Northcott. Chicago, IL: University of Chicago Press, 1988.

North, John A. *Roman Religion*. Oxford: Oxford University Press, 2000.

Oakes, Lorna, and Lucia Gahlin. *The Mysteries of Ancient Egypt: An Illustrated Reference to the Myths, Religions, Pyramids and Temples of the Land of the Pharaohs*. London: Lorenz, 2004.

Orlin, Eric M. *Temples, Religion, and Politics in the Roman Republic*. Leiden, Netherlands: E.J. Brill, 1997.

Pelikan, Jaroslav J. *Jesus Through the Centuries: His Place in the History of Culture*. New Haven, CT: Yale University Press, 1985.

Pemberton, Delia, and Joann Fletcher. *Treasures of the Pharaohs: The Glories of Ancient Egypt*. London: Duncan Baird, 2004.

Peters, Francis E. *Muhammad and the Origins of Islam*. Albany, NY: SUNY Press, 1994.

Porter, Barbara Nevling, ed. *One God or Many?: Concepts of Divinity in the Ancient World*. Chebeague, ME: Casco Bay Assyriological Institute, 2000.

Pritchard, James B., ed. *The Ancient Near East: An Anthology of Texts and Pictures*, 2vols. Princeton, NJ: Princeton University Press, 1975.

Prosecky, J. ed. *Intellectual Life of the Ancient Near East*. Prague: Academy of Sciences of the Czech Republic, Oriental Literature, 1998.

Redford, Donald. *Akhenaten: The Heretic King*. Princeton, NJ: Princeton University Press, 1987.

_____. *The Ancient Gods Speak: A Guide to Egyptian Religion*. Oxford: Oxford University Press, 2002.

Reynolds, Frank E., and David Tracy, eds. *Religion and Practical Reason: New Essays in the Comparative Philosophy of Religions*. Albany, NY: State University of New York Press, 1994.

Richards, Janet E. *Society and Death in Ancient Egypt: Mortuary Landscapes Of The Middle Kingdom*. Cambridge/New York: Cambridge University Press, 2005.

Rodinson, Maxime. *The Arabs*. Chicago, IL: University of Chicago Press, 1981.

_____. *Muhammad*, 2nd ed. London: Penguin Books, 1996.

Rose, Jenny. *The Image of Zoroaster: The Persian Mage Through European Eyes*. New York: Bibliotheca Persica Press, 2000.

_____. *Zoroastrianism: An Introduction*. London: I.B. Tauris, 2011.

Russell, David Syme. *The Jews from Alexander to Herod*. Oxford: Oxford University Press, 1967.

Sanders, E. P. *Paul and Palestinian Judaism*. Philadelphia, PA: Fortress Press, 1977.

_____. *Jesus and Judaism*. Philadelphia, PA: Fortress Press, 1985.

Sanders, E. P. and Margaret Davies. *Studying the Synoptic Gospels*. Philadelphia, PA: Trinity Press International, 1989.

Sasson, Jack M., ed. *Civilizations of the Ancient Near East*. 2 vols. Peabody, MA: Hendrickson Publishers, 2000.

Sauneron, Serge. *The Priests of Ancient Egypt*. Ithaca, NY: Cornell University Press, 2000.

Scheid, John. *An Introduction to Roman Religion*. Translated by Janet Lloyd. Edinburgh: Edinburgh University Press, 2003.

Schimmel, Annemarie. *And Muhammad is His Messenger: The Veneration of the Prophet in Islamic Piety*. Chapel Hill, NC: University of North Carolina Press, 1985.

_____. *Mystical Dimensions of Islam*. Chapel Hill, NC: University of North Carolina Press, 1975.

Schlerath, Bernfried, ed. *Zarathustra*. Wege der Forschung 169. Darmstadt: Wissenschaftliche Buchgesellschaft, 1970.

Schuon, Frithjof. *The Transcendent Unity of Religions*. Rev. ed. New York: Harper & Row, 1975.

Seebass, Horst. *Mose und Aaron, Sinai und Gottesberg*. Abhandlungen zur evangelischen Theologie 2. Bonn: Bouvier, 1962.

Sharon, Moshe, ed. *Studies in Modern Religions and Religious Movements and the Babi-Baha'i Faiths*. Leiden, the Netherlands, and Boston: Brill, 2004.

Sharpe, Eric J. *Comparative Religion. A History*, 2nd ed. La Salle, IL.: Open Court Press, 1986.

Shaw, Ian. *Ancient Egypt: A Very Short Introduction*. Oxford/New York: Oxford University Press, 2004.

Shin, Hyeon Woo. *Textual Criticism and the Synoptic Problem in Historical Jesus Research: The Search for Valid Criteria*. Leuven, Belgium: Peeters, 2004.

Smith, Jonathan Z. *Relating Religion: Essays in the Study of Religion*. Chicago, IL: University of Chicago Press, 2004.

Smith, Mark S. *The Early History of God: Yahweh and the Other Deities in Ancient Israel*. 2d ed. Grand Rapids: Eerdmans, 2002.

Smith, Morton. *Jesus the Magician*. New York, NY: Harper & Row, 1978.

Smith, Peter. *The Babi and Baha'i Religions: From Messianic Shi'ism to a*

World Religion. Cambridge, MA: Cambridge University Press, 1987.

_____. *The Baha'i Faith: A Short History.* Oxford: Oneworld, 1996.

Smith, Wilfred Cantwell. *The Meaning and End of Religion.* New York: Mentor Books, 1962.

Snell, Daniel C. ed. *A Companion to the Ancient Near East.* Malden, MA: Blackwell Publishing Ltd. 2005, 2007.

_____. *Life in the Ancient Near East, 3100–332 BC.* New Haven, CT: Yale University Press, 1997.

Stanton, Graham. *The Gospels and Jesus,* 2nd ed. New York: Oxford University Press, 2002.

Stegemann, Hartmut. *The Library of Qumran, on the Essenes, Qumran, John the Baptist, and Jesus.* Grand Rapids, MI: W. B. Eerdmans, 1998.

Stemberger, Gunther. *Jewish Contemporaries of Jesus: Pharisees, Sadducees, Essenes,* translated by Allan W. Mahnke. Minneapolis MN: Fortress Press, 1995.

Swidler, Leonard J., and Paul Mojzes. *The Study of Religion in an Age of Global Dialogue.* Philadelphia, PA: Temple University Press, 2000.

Takacs, Sarolta A. *Isis and Sarapis in the Roman World,* Vol. 124. Leiden: The Netherlands: E.J. Brill, 1995.

Tardieu, Michel. *Manichaeism,* translated by M.B. DeBevoise. Urbana & Chicago: University of Illinois Press, 2008.

Tatlock, Jason, ed. *The Middle East: Its History and Culture.* Bethesda, MD: University Press of Maryland, 2012.

Taylor, J. Glen. *Yahweh and the Sun: Biblical and Archaeological Evidence for Sun Worship in Ancient Israel.* Sheffield: JSOT Press, 1993.

Taylor, John H. *Death and the Afterlife in Ancient Egypt.* London: British Museum Press, 2001.

Theissen, Gerd. *The Historical Jesus: A Comprehensive Guide.* Minneapolis, MN: Fortress Press, 1998.

Tyldesley, Joyce A. *Judgement of the Pharaoh: Crime and Punishment in Ancient Egypt.* London: Weidenfeld and Nicholson, 2000.

Ulansey, David. *The Origins of the Mithraic Mysteries: Cosmology and Salvation in the Ancient World.* New York and Oxford: Oxford University Press, 1989.

Van de Mieroop, Marc. *A History of the Ancient Near East (ca. 3000–323 BC),* 2nd ed. Malden, MA: Blackwell, 2004.

Van der Leeuw, Gerhardus. *Religion in Essence and Manifestation: A Study in Phenomenology.* London: G. Allen & Unwin, 1938.

Van Seeters, John. *The Life of Moses. The Yahwist as Historian in Exodus-Numbers.* Louisville, KY: Westminster/John Knox Press, 1994.

Varenne, Jean. *Zoroastre.* Paris: Editions Seghers 1975.

Vermaseren, Maarten Jozef. *Cybele and Attis: The Myth and the Cult.* London: Thames and Hudson, 1977.

Vincent, Ken R. *The Magi: From Zoroaster to "The Three Wise Men"*. North Richland Hills, TX: BIBAL Press, 1999.

Watson, Alan. *The State, Law, and Religion: Pagan Rome*. Athens, GA: University of Georgia Press, 1992.

Watt, William Montgomery. *Muhammad: Prophet and Statesman*. London: Oxford University Press, 1961.

Weaver, Walter P. *Jesus and His Biographers*. The Dead Sea Scrolls and Christian Origins Library, vol. 7. North Richland Hills, TX: BIBAL Press, 2005.

White, L. Michael. *From Jesus to Christianity*. San Francisco, CA: HarperSanFrancisco, 2004.

Wulff, David M. *Psychology of Religion : Classic and Contemporary Views*. New York: John Wiley & Sons, 1991.

Yamauchi, Edwin M. *Persia and the Bible*. Grand Rapids, MI: Baker Book House, 1990.

Zaehner, Robert C. *The Dawn and Twilight of Zoroastrianism*. New York: Putnam, 1961.

_____. *The Teachings of the Magi: A Compendium of Zoroastrian Beliefs*. New York: Oxford University Press 1956; reprint 1976.

Zakaria, Rafiq. *Muhammad and the Qur'an*. New York: Penguin, 1991.

Zeitlin, Irving, M. *The Historical Muhammad*. Cambridge, UK: Polity Press, 2007.

_____. *Jesus and the Judaism of His Time*. Cambridge, UK: Polity Press, 1988.

Index